Beer,
Booze, and
Books

Beer, Booze, and Books

... a sober look at

higher education

By Jim Matthews

Viaticum Press

Peterborough, New Hampshire
Corvalis, Oregon

VIATICUM PRESS

Peterborough, NH—Corvallis, OR

Editor: Margaret Allyson
Book and Cover Design: David Nelson
Cover Photography: Comstock

For additional copies contact:
Jim Matthews
27 West Ridge Drive
Peterborough, NH 03458
(603) 924-6817
http://www.beerboozebooks.com
bbbjim@monad.net

Printed in Canada

ISBN-0-9631834-1-9

Dedicated to
Mom and Dad.
Thanks.

Acknowledgements

I'd like to express my thanks and appreciation to all the concerned students across the country whose forthright contributions have made this book what it is - an honest look at the impact of alcohol and other drug use on college students. In particular, the students of Keene State College have provided me with valuable insights into the problems and concerns of college students. They continue to make my daily alcohol education and abuse prevention work interesting, enjoyable and inspiring.

Special thanks go to the Prevention Research Institute, especially Ray Daugherty and Terry O'Bryan. Their "Prime for Life" program and the "Lifestyle Risk Reduction Process" have provided effective abuse prevention strategies for not only college students but children and adults alike. Much of the information in this book regarding the risks for impairment problems and the development of addiction is based on their dedicated work throughout the country. Their permission to use this material is greatly appreciated.

The Core Institute, the Higher Education Center and the Harvard School of Public Health continue to provide college prevention specialists with valuable program support and critical data regarding campus alcohol issues. Their professional work is appreciated by all of us who are conducting campus prevention programs. Other folks whose support and inspiration I sincerely appreciate are Dr. Will Keim, from Oregon State University, Dr. Delina Hickey, former Vice President for Student Affairs at Keene State College, Carole Middlebrooks from the University of Georgia, Mona Anderson and Peter Lake. A very special thank you goes to Denis, Mary, Mairead and Ryan. ♦

Table of Contents

Table of Contents

Table of Contents

Addiction

Introduction

" **I** DON'T WANT THE TIME OF MY LIFE to ruin the rest of my life." Those words of wisdom were spoken by a student who entered my office depressed over the fact that alcohol use was taking over his life. While in high school he was an honor student and outstanding athlete. Now a college sophomore, he had been dismissed from his team and his grades were the worst they had ever been. He was now looking for help.

The difficulties experienced by college students due to high risk alcohol consumption are often a result of serious misunderstandings about its use. "I'll quit when I graduate... It's part of college life... Everyone does it... It was just a game... It's only beer... There's nuthin' else to do." These are all-too-familiar phrases reflecting the beliefs and attitudes expressed by many college students attempting to justify, in some way, their high risk alcohol use.

"Beer, Booze, and Books" can help you, the college student, gain a clearer understanding of the role alcohol may be playing in your life or the lives of your peers. Included in this book are numerous quotes taken from the thousands of students I have worked with during the past fifteen years. These quotes indicate the myriad of difficulties and, at times, misperceptions and inaccurate information that influence students when they make decisions about alcohol use. At the request of some of the students, some of the quotes have been either adapted or listed as anonymous to protect their identity.

As you will see, there is no clear cut answer to the dilemma about alcohol use. What we do know is that alcohol use can be risky. What we do know is that although most students either do not drink, or if they do choose to drink they do so at a low risk level, there is a high profile minority of other students drinking heavily and suffering because it. Some of the results may be hangovers, vomiting, or missing class. Other negative outcomes may include poor grades, fights or unplanned sexual encounters resulting in sexually transmitted diseases. The high risk use of alcohol by these students is also problematic for their peers who do not consume at a risky level—late night noise in the residence halls, fights, and property damage are just some of the problems they face.

It has been six years since the First Edition of this book. During that time there has been no significant change with regard to the overall drinking patterns of college students despite the numerous programs developed to challenge this serious problem. One promising strategy is referred to as "social norming." The emphasis of this strategy is to reinforce for students an understanding that most students either do not drink or, if they do drink, they do so at a low risk level. Throughout this book I have attempted to reinforce this fact by providing you with accurate data that suports this belief and resulting strategy.

However, since we know that approximately 80 percent of college students drink, I believe it is imperative that you receive clear, accurate and applicable information. Too often college students dismiss alcohol education programs as judgmental preaching based on scare tactics and moralistic lectures. Regrettably, these students are often correct in their evaluation of these programs. While neither condoning nor condemning alcohol consumption, this book will take a closer look at college drinking and provide you with insights which will help you minimize your risks, if you do choose to consume alcohol.

Finally, the choice to consume alcohol or not is *your* choice—not the host of the party, not the social chair of the fraternity, not your roommate, not your friend, not the captain of the team. The choice to consume or not and the choice of how much if you do consume are yours and yours alone. These are choices you will be confronted with throughout your college life. I hope this book helps you in making the choices that will make college "the time of your life"—a time you will not regret but will cherish the rest of your life.

♦

Party Time

... where the action is!

"Most people could not understand why I would go to a party if I did not intend to drink. This shows that many people probably go to parties for the sole purpose of getting drunk."

Jason R., University of Massachusetts, senior

"I usually have just two or three drinks at a party. I really do not understand why some people get so trashed."

Allen B., Brown University, sophomore

"Getting wasted is what it's all about."

John J., University of Oregon, sophomore

ACCORDING TO WEBSTER'S NEW WORLD DICTIONARY a party is "a gathering to which guests are invited in order to enjoy one another's company." Sooner or later most college students find themselves at a campus party. It might be a full-blown kegger in a friend's dingy basement or a tightly managed gathering sponsored by a liability-conscious fraternity. Maybe it'll be a small get-together in a residence hall where people play board games and have quiet conversation. Then again, it might be an off-campus party where pot, LSD, mushrooms, ecstasy or maybe some cocaine will be available.

Most students who attend campus parties consume alcohol and yet, despite the exaggerated representations in the mass media, most of them drink at a low risk level. However, many others do drink to impairment, getting drunk and putting themselves and others at risk for a variety of possible difficulties. As part of an alcohol-education program on my campus, students are challenged to attend a party and abstain from alcohol. *Below is a composite of excerpts from over four hundred reports by students who attended numerous different parties but did not consume alcohol. The excerpts provide both the male and the female perspective.* Some students had a great time, but for others it was a difficult experience. Many were pressured to drink, while others were respected for their choice to abstain. All found this challenge quite revealing. By the way, the quotes from these students have not been edited!

9:00 PM:
When I arrived at the door I resented being screened by the guys. You're looked over to make sure you are "good enough." However, I have never heard of a girl being rejected, as the saying goes, "If you have a chest you'll get in."

The whole place smelled of stale beer and alcohol and the floor was one giant puddle of beer topped off with old broken plastic beer cups.

Party Time

I watched my friends go immediately to the keg. They didn't even stop to see who was there or to socialize for a couple of minutes. At first I thought this was funny, but then I realized after watching the door for awhile that just about everyone who walked in went straight for the keg. They saved their "hellos" until after their beers were safely in their hands. It was almost as if they needed the beer to socialize.

They were offering beer, mixed drinks, shots, basically all types of alcohol but nothing that was non-alcoholic. I really resented that.

10:00 PM:
I was not really surprised by what I first saw. It was about 10:00 P.M. so it was still early. Not many of the hundred or so people there had much to drink yet, so things were relatively quiet. Not long after that though, that is, two or three beers later, people began to loosen up.

When we reached the basement the stench of beer and cigarettes filled the air. It was funny that all three of us noticed the same thing. Everyone reeked of alcohol. People were piled up in front of the kegs waiting impatiently for their beers. Nasty words were being exchanged between a number of people. We laughed at the thought of not having to be stuck between all those sweaty strangers.

I felt out of place because I was the only one not holding a beer. As the night went along I felt less out of place because people were finally accepting the fact that I was not drinking.

Everyone accepted the fact that I wasn't going to drink and we all had fun nonetheless. They realized that just cause I wasn't drunk it didn't mean that I couldn't have fun with them.

There were groups of guys by the kegs that were having drinking contests to see who could drink the most the fastest.

11:00 PM:
The lines for the girls' rooms were outrageous and once inside they made you sick. Who knows what those drunk girls did in there to make it smell so bad.

I was really falling apart and was not enjoying it. All the drunk people kept bumping into me and getting on my nerves. I wasn't thinking of hitting anyone but I was considering hitting the bottle and putting this project off for another night.

The thing that killed me the most was how rude everyone was to each other. There was a person passed out in the corner and I guess nobody moved him because he looked so comfortable.

I was having fun watching everyone slur and spit on each other.

I didn't appreciate trying to talk to someone and have them spit in my face. I needed to escort my friend to the bathroom every five minutes. I was embarrassed to be standing next to her when she flirted with a total stranger—a stranger I know she never would have given a second look if she wasn't drunk. I guess the "beer goggles" were taking over.

They would laugh at things that I didn't find at all funny.

People pushed and shoved me all night without saying sorry or excuse me.

I walked into the bathroom and someone was taking a leak in the shower.

I went over to my friends and began to dance with them. It was actually more fun without alcohol because I wasn't spilling beer all over myself. But, I just had to accept the fact that others were going to spill beer on me anyway.

As many people got intoxicated, they seemed to feel uncomfortable interacting with me, a sober person. As the night went on fewer and fewer intoxicated people came to talk to me.

> Following an evening of heavy consumption, Nero and his drinking buddies in Imperial Rome would beat up citizens for fun, did damage to private property and engaged in drunken brawls that endangered life and limb. Nero loved to push his companions into open sewer holes.

Midnight:

I usually thought the guys were the loud, obnoxious ones. But some of the girls were even worse than the guys. The party was getting really loud because everyone was trying to talk over everyone else and the music too. I don't think I listened to

Party Time

a conversation that didn't include plenty of profanity. Some of the sexual tones of the conversations were actually quite disgusting and they sounded quite sexist too.

I had a great time talking to people and dancing. I liked the feeling of being in control of my actions. I stayed at the party and had a good time. It was a pleasant change for me.

Another thing I noticed was how hostile people became. Both males and females were getting in what seemed to be very violent moods. It seemed like a couple of guys wanted to start a fight with anyone who walked by them. Girls spoke about grudges they had with other girls.

At midnight I was totally bored, sick of getting bumped into, spilled on and tired of listening to these intoxicated people spouting a bunch of bull.

The thing that got me was the beer dumping. Two boys within an hour decided to come up to me, look me straight in the face and proceeded to dump beer down the front of my blouse. If they were that curious as to the size of my chest all they needed to do was ask. I do think though that if I was drunk I would have viewed it as funny.

I felt like leaving early. It seemed like I was weighing down everyone's good time. I just didn't think all that was happening was so funny.

Something that struck me funny was watching my drunk brothers and friends trying to scoop. They try so hard and most of the time get shot down. I saw one scoop this girl and I know when they woke up they both were going to wish she would have shot him down. I saw him the next morning and asked him how his night went. He laughed and just walked away. Girls are not so bad because they usually arrive and leave with their friends. They watch out for each other.

The bathrooms were horrible. Of course there was no toilet paper—so my girlfriends and I needed to drip dry.

1:00 AM:
Many couples were leaving, ones that had either just met that night or had known each other from a party or two ago.

As the night moved on I was grabbed and prodded by drunk guys. I usually don't say anything about this stuff if I'm drinking. But I saw this guy actually put his hand up a girl's skirt. I stopped to think about it and realized that when I drink and let someone paw at me I am really degrading myself.

The guys and girls alike were wearing their "beer goggles" and checking each other out. What begins as a night out with friends turns into a "scooping fest." Drunk guys would come up to us and begin to tell us meaningless things about their manhood and why we should go home with them.

All I wanted to do was drink or get high and the rest of the night went the same until I met a girl and left with her. No, I didn't scoop her I just walked her home. It was a cool way to end the night. I think the fact that I was sober impressed her. I've already gone out with her twice and think this could be the start of something new.

My friend stayed at the party with some guy. I tried to get her to leave but she insisted she was OK. It really scared me to leave her in that place but what could I do?

By one o'clock our clothes were covered with beer. At this point we wanted a beer just so we could deal with the idiots.

2:00 AM:
It seemed as though it was now the designated pickup hour. Girls were working on guys and guys on girls. If someone was shot down they would move on to the next one. At this point people seemed to have lowered their standards.

Often it's in the early hours of the morning when violence may occur. Fights seem to be ready to break out all over the place. Most of the time these fights are over the most ridiculous reasons. One excuse this night was "He kept staring at me."

We ended up leaving the party a little early because we thought the atmosphere was turning into one of those "hooking up" ones. Guys and girls were dirty dancing and kissing and we knew some didn't know each other before the night started.

Finally my friends decided they wanted to leave mainly because the beer ran out. I was never so happy to get out of there. I helped my friends stumble home and wondered how I usually make it home safely. I guess I've been lucky.

3:00 AM:
I noticed this girl leaving or should I say being carried home. She had writing all

over her. When you pass out people do crazy things to you. She was lucky it was only some silly scribbling.

I escorted three of my drunk friends home. Dodging the RAs and security was a memory. When I got back to the comfort of my room I realized I brought the party home with me—I stunk! I went in to take a shower and found two of my friends throwing up.

People had real bad attitudes when the beer ran out at three in the morning. I was thinking to myself, "Damn, these guys have been here for five hours, can barely walk and they want more beer." But I know I'm the same way when I'm drunk. I know I probably shouldn't drink another drop but I still run my mouth. Trying to kick people out after the beer was gone was a real chore. People just didn't want to leave because they thought there was a "hush" keg.

The Next Day:
When I woke up after a good night's sleep, I felt terrific and headache free. It was a memorable experience. I kept thinking "I hope I don't get like they did, but I'm sure I have." That is a very troubling thought.

This made me realize that every beer brings more danger to the drinker. I cannot say I will never drink at a party again but I think I will be more careful now. Being on the sober side made me realize the dangers of being on the drunken side and this awareness will hopefully help me in the future.

I'm sure many of my friends were jealous that I was able to get up early, go mountain biking, have a picnic with two friends and come home to study for Monday's exam.

It really annoys me when I go to a party and not drink but wake up the next morning feeling like I'm hungover because my hair smells so much like smoke.

By not drinking that night, it positively changed my whole weekend. I didn't sleep away the next day. I got some school work done. The usual "Sunday depression" didn't effect me.

I was appalled by the behavior but what bothered me even more was thinking that maybe I acted the same way they did when I am drinking.

I woke up without a hangover. My friends were dragging around feeling the effects of last night's drinking. One of my friends said to me, "Wow, I can't believe you don't have a hangover. You were having so much fun dancing and laughing. You must have been trashed." I realized how sad that comment was. She did not know that what she was saying was that you can't have fun without alcohol. I shook my head and walked away.

Party Risks

As you can tell by the experiences of these students, attending a campus party can be fun. It can also be an extremely high risk activity. There are risks taken not only by the drinkers but also by all those involved in the party:

- The drinkers risk an injury from a fight or a fall. They also risk acquaintance rape or the spread of AIDS or other sexually transmitted diseases due to impaired judgment. An alcohol-related car crash is another risk. At the very least, many may spend the morning "talking to God through the great white telephone" during a mean, painful hangover.

- Hosts risk lawsuits from drinkers who may be injured or from those injured by the drinkers. There's also a strong probability of property damage to their residence.

- Non-drinkers risk being involved in any of the aforementioned scenarios just by simply "being there."

- Colleges and universities continue to be at risk for possible lawsuits if the hosts of the parties are in some way affiliated with the institution.

Is "party" a noun or a verb? When we hear someone say, "I'm going to really party tonight," more often than not it means "I'm going to get really trashed tonight." On the campus today, "to party" is now synonymous with "to get drunk or to get high on other drugs." Therefore students set themselves up for a self-fulfilling prophecy: "If I'm going to party, I'm going to get wasted." Later in this book we will look at some strategies for attending parties and enjoying yourself while minimizing your risk for an alcohol-related problem. In the meantime, let's take a look at this stuff called alcohol. ◆

Personal Challenge: Party Observations

Goal:

To raise awareness of the behaviors of college students at a party where alcohol is being consumed.

Instructions:

1. Attend a campus or off-campus party where alcohol will be served.
2. Do not consume alcohol.
3. Observe the behaviors of the participants. What are they like early in the party? What are they like later in the party? Do people try to get you to drink?
4. Observe your own behaviors while at the party.

Reflections:

a. How did you feel at the party?
b. Can you have fun at a party without drinking?
c. How do you handle pressure from your peers to drink? What can you do to minimize the impact of peer pressure?
d. How well do you socialize with others at a party if you do not drink?
e. What was the impact of alcohol on the atmosphere of the party? on you?

Chapter Two

Alcohol

... odorless, colorless, tasteless and potentially dangerous.

"I love the feeling it gives me."
> Jessica J., Franklin Pierce College senior

I hate the feeling of being out of control."
> Steve L., University of Florida junior

"I hate the taste of beer but I drink it anyway."
> Jessica L., University of Florida sophomore

"It acts as liquid courage and a social lubricant."
> Alan S., University of New Hampshire sophomore

Alcohol

BEER, WINE AND LIQUOR ALL CONTAIN ALCOHOL—pure ethyl alcohol (ETOH), which is odorless, colorless and tasteless. Alcohol is one of the most enigmatic products we consume today. Historically, it has been with us since the Stone Age; the Bible alludes to Noah's getting drunk; it was a staple on the *Mayflower* as it crossed the Atlantic to America. Grandfathers share their beer with toddlers sitting on their knees while mothers tell their children to wait until they're of legal age before they drink. By some it's considered the devil's brew, yet others use it in sacred ritual. It has survived temperance movements in Italy, Germany, England and the United States. It's been used as a thirst quencher, to relieve hunger, as a medication and as a mind-altering drug. It's heavily regulated yet the regulations are often disregarded either secretly or overtly. On the college campus it is the main attraction at fraternity keggers and at faculty sherry hours. On a national level college student alcohol consumption averages apparoximately 34 gallons of alcoholic beverages per year[1] or some four hundred billion cans of beer, averaging 55 six packs apiece.[2] The media consistently highlights the dangerous and damaging behaviors of a number of students whose drinking is negatively impacting their own success as well as disrupting the lives of the students around them. Yet, interestingly, despite the disturbing headlines and news reports of excessive drinking on today's campuses, the reality is that most college students either do not drink or drink in a low risk manner. (The importance of a clear understanding about the true nature of college drinking patterns will be presented later in this book.) In the meantime, let's take a look at what happens to us once we have consumed this popular drug called alcohol.

Path

"I always thought that you drink, get a buzz, maybe a hangover and that's it. I couldn't believe how much alcohol affects so many parts of the body. God, what have I done to myself?"

John H., Keene State College senior

If you choose to drink alcohol while you are in college, it is important that you understand the impact alcohol can have on your body and mind. When you have a drink, up to 5 percent of the alcohol is absorbed into your bloodstream through the capillaries in your mouth. Then, approximately 20 percent is absorbed into the bloodstream through the stomach lining. The remainder is absorbed into the bloodstream through the walls of the small intestine. While traveling through the bloodstream, the alcohol affects all the organs it encounters, especially the brain.

Blood Alcohol Level

"We got her to the hospital just in time. Later we heard that her BAL was .41 percent."

Ralph S., Manhattan College junior

Blood alcohol level (BAL) refers to the ratio of alcohol to blood in the bloodstream. It also accurately reflects the level of alcohol in the entire body. BAL, also known as blood alcohol concentration (BAC), is represented as a percentage. Here's an analogy which may help you understand what those numbers represent. Picture this—a shelf with 10,000 compartments. Each compartment is filled with a drop of blood. If I replace one drop of blood with one drop of alcohol, the shelf now has a BAL of .01 percent. If I replace two drops of blood with two drops of alcohol, the shelf now has a BAL of .02 percent. If I replace ten drops of blood with ten drops of alcohol, then the shelf has a BAL of .10 percent.

Previously a BAL of .10 percent was considered legally drunk in most states. National legislation in the year 2000 has proposed a national BAL limit of .08 percent—and rightly so. After all, ongoing research continues to indicate a clear, direct relationship between increased BAL and increased risk for automobile crashes, serious injury and death.

In the 1800s some tavern keepers kept smoked and heavily salted codfish in kegs next to their barrels of booze, encouraging customers to help themselves freely and without charge. The codfish, of course, engendered a mighty thirst, which could only be quenched with generous helpings of ale or rum.

Alcohol

Metabolism

> *"I had no idea what to do with the funnel. All I know is we drank a lot of beer through that thing. I got shit-faced in less than an hour."*
>
> Stacey R., Keene State College first-year student

> *"Often times when I go to parties I will drink for a little while and then start drinking water around 11 or 12. I'll do this because I feel myself getting drunk. This gives me time to sober up."*
>
> John R., SUNY Cortland sophomore

Alcohol is a toxin. The liver has the job of metabolizing or breaking down and clearing toxins, such as alcohol, from the body. It can do this at an average rate of approximately one drink per hour. (A "drink" will be defined shortly.) If you drink more than one drink per hour, the alcohol accumulates in your bloodstream, increasing your BAL and increasing your impairment. A simple analogy to help you understand this is a faucet and a sink. If I turn the water on slowly, it simply drains through the sink. If I turn the water on more quickly, it will accumulate in the sink. It's the same with alcohol. If we sip it slowly it gets metabolized and "drains away" through the body before it can accumulate in the bloodstream.

One very dangerous activity popular on many campuses has been using a funnel to consume multiple beers or other drinks in a very short time—a few seconds, as a matter of fact! One reason this is dangerous is that using a funnel or, for that matter, chugging, or shot-gunning beers circumvents the body's natural protection system. This protection consists of a valve between our stomach and small intestine called the pyloric valve. Most times this valve will close if our BAL gets too high, thus causing us to vomit. But when we consume a large quantity of alcohol in a short period of time, the valve does not have a chance to close. Our BAL is then allowed to climb dangerously high.

Although the average rate of metabolism is one drink per hour, the range is approximately one-half drink to one-and-a-half drinks per hour. This is important to remember if you use one of those educational CD ROMs or pre-calculated BAL charts like the one at the end of this chapter. The estimated BAL indicated on the CD ROM or chart is usually based on the average metabolic rate of one drink per hour. Therefore, if your metabolism happens to be slow, your BAL could be almost 50 percent higher than indicated on the chart!

Impairment

> *"I know a lot of people who think, 'why drink if you're not going to get drunk?' I used to think this way, but what is so great about getting drunk, getting sick, passing out or putting yourself in danger?"*
>
> Deborah A., Plymouth State College junior

> *"I try to be a responsible drinker. Most of the time I don't get really drunk, I just get a good buzz."*
>
> Buddy S., University of Virginia sophomore

As we just saw, if you drink alcohol at a rate faster than one drink per hour, your blood alcohol level will increase with each drink. The greater your BAL, the greater the level of impairment. Impairment is any slowing of our physical, psychological or emotional functioning beyond the initial relaxation effect of alcohol.[3] The greater the level of impairment, the greater the risk for an impairment problem. The following scenario represents the typical development of impairment due to alcohol consumption by an average 175-pound male (Joe) and a 125-pound female (Jane) after drinking for three or four hours.

- Before heading out to a party, Joe and Jane may feel a little shy, insecure or stressed about socializing in a new environment, with new people. They decide to have a "primer." After one drink, Joe will have a BAL of approximately .02 percent, and Jane's will be approximately .037 percent. There will be little change in their behavior, but they may feel more relaxed.

- As they arrive at the party, they may still feel uptight, so they head straight for the keg. Within the next hour or so they consume three or four drinks each. Jane's BAL will be about .12 percent, and Joe's approximately .06 percent. They are high or "buzzed." Joe has lost his inhibitions, and it is obvious he has been drinking. Jane may start to slur her speech and stagger a bit. Her reaction time and dexterity are severely impaired.

- They might join a drinking game and lose a couple of rounds. After six drinks, they are obviously impaired. Even though their bodies are metabolizing the alcohol, their livers cannot keep up with the amount being consumed. Therefore their BALs continue to rise. Jane's is around .19 percent, and her emotions are becoming erratic. Joe, with an approximate BAL of .11

percent, might now be slurring his speech and staggering. Surprisingly though, they may not even recognize they are impaired.

- They feel daring and funnel a few beers. They now have consumed ten drinks each. Jane is nearing a coma with an approximate BAL of .30 percent. Joe is experiencing erratic mood swings and is becoming belligerent. His BAL is about .20 percent.

- Friends might convince them to leave the party and go back to their residence hall. Before he leaves, Joe hits the shot bar and guzzles five shots of liquor. His BAL now approaches .30 percent. If they kept drinking, they would depress their central nervous systems dramatically. Their respiratory and/or circulatory systems could fail. Both could come dangerously close to a coma and possible death.

- Their judgment and inhibitions are depressed. They may attempt to have sex, and new risks then arise. Is there mutual consent to have sex? Will Joe be able to attain an erection? Will Jane be able to achieve an orgasm? What about the long-term emotional impact of this unplanned sexual encounter? Who's got the condom? Will they use it?

The reactions indicated in the above scenario are generalizations. Some people would have been more impaired more quickly, and others would have required more alcohol to become so impaired. We will see shortly that tolerance and a number of other factors will determine the impact alcohol could have on you during any session of drinking. These factors include weight, gender, food, altitude, health and age.

Tolerance

> *"I usually drink two to three times per week and usually these times I get impaired. I now can handle two six-packs without getting impaired. I know that I am not making good decisions but I enjoy drinking. It makes you feel good for awhile but then it brings you way down."*
>
> Barbara U., University of New Hampshire sophomore

People drink alcohol for a variety of reasons—to quench their thirst, for flavor, for sacred ritual, for celebration. Many people, especially college students, drink to get

After Buffalo Bill Cody the famous frontiersman was convinced by a friend he was drinking too much bourbon, he swore a solemn oath he would limit himself to a single glass per day. Unfortunately, being held to his vow made Cody melancholy, nervous and irascible. But he did not want to go back on his word. A friend found the ideal solution by giving Cody a glass snifter holding a quart of the red essence. Thus Buffalo Bill could keep his word and enjoy his usual generous measure.

impaired. If you start drinking, it may take you two or three drinks to get impaired. If you continue drinking to impairment on a regular basis, each time you drink you will need a little more alcohol to reach the same level of impairment because your body will have adapted due to the previous drinking episode. In other words, the body has increased its tolerance to alcohol.

Here's why: Our bodies are wonderful machines. They adapt very well. Take for instance the body's ability to adapt to varying temperatures. As we live through a warm summer, our bodies adapt to the warmer temperatures. When a cool September day hits us—say around 50 degrees—we would normally put on a jacket. Our bodies adapted to the warmer temperatures of summer and are not accustomed to the colder fall temperatures. Then, during a very cold winter, our bodies adapt to the cold. When spring arrives with an occasional warmer day—around 50 degrees—students around the campus will be wearing T-shirts and shorts! Their bodies have adapted to winter and can tolerate colder temperatures.[4]

It's the same with alcohol. Tolerance is the degree to which your body has adapted to a given blood alcohol level. Each time you drink to impairment, your tolerance will increase; your body will try to minimize your impairment at a given BAL. To get impaired again, it will take just a bit more alcohol to overcome the adaptation. The level of adaptation or increase in tolerance is subtle and not easily measured. Research indicates, however, that in just one session of drinking, your body will probably have a slight increase in tolerance. We see that the level of impairment for a given BAL is higher as the BAL is increasing compared to the impairment when the BAL is diminishing.

If you stop drinking to impairment for a few weeks, your tolerance will then decrease. For instance, the tolerance for many students fluctuates as their school circumstances change. They may begin school in September and have fairly low tolerance. Maybe three or four beers get them impaired. As the semester continues and they continue drinking to impairment each weekend, their tolerance will increase. They may go home for winter break and decrease their consumption. As a result, their tolerance may subside a bit. But once they return to school in January, back to the bars and parties and increased alcohol consumption, their tolerance will continue to rise again. When summer rolls around, maybe they will return home to their parents. They may work at a full-time job or hang around with their non-college friends who tend to drink less than they do. Their consumption decreases, therefore their tolerance once again begins to decrease.

But remember increased tolerance only delays impairment, it cannot prevent it. Whenever we drink to impairment, we are at greater risk for impairment problems such as falls, fights, DUI infractions or car crashes, unplanned sexual encounters and the like.

Other Considerations

In addition to the amount of alcohol consumed, the speed at which it is consumed and your tolerance, a number of other factors will also affect how quickly and to what degree you will get impaired if you choose to drink:

- Food in the stomach will slow the absorption of alcohol into the bloodstream and delay impairment. The *type* of food ingested (carbohydrate, fat, protein) has not been shown to have a measurable influence on BAL. However, we do know that the larger the meal and the closer the time between eating and drinking, the lower the peak blood alcohol concentration. Studies have shown reductions in peak blood alcohol concentration (as opposed to those of a fasting individual under otherwise similar circumstances) of between 9 percent and 23 percent.

- Alcohol mixed with carbonated beverages such as Coca-Cola or Seven Up will be absorbed more quickly into the bloodstream. This is also true for champagne and wine coolers.

- Women who are pre-menstrual and sometimes those on birth control pills tend to get more impaired more quickly.

- Strong emotions—anger, fear, loneliness—tend to hasten impairment.

- If you are tired, sick or just getting over an illness, you tend to get more impaired more quickly.

- Mixing alcohol with other drugs often leads to increased impairment in a shorter period of time. ♦

Alcohol

Personal Challenge: Estimating BAL

Goal:
To learn how to estimate Blood Alcohol Level.

Instructions:
To estimate BAL:
- move down the Drink/Weight Index chart on the following page to the number of drinks and your gender. (A drink equals a12 oz. regular beer, 1 oz. shot of 100 proof liquor, 1.5 oz. shot of 80 proof liquor, or 4 oz. glass of regular table wine)
- move across the chart to your weight to arrive at your Drink/Weight Index
- subtract .01% from the Drink/Weight Index for each hour from the start of the drinking to the point in time you want to measure the BAL.

Exercise 1: John weighs 200 pounds and is 22 years old. He is out at a party and has been drinking shots and beers. He had five shots (1 ounce of 100 proof whiskey) and a twelve ounce bottle of beer after each shot. He has been drinking at the party for three hours. The host suggested he quit drinking alcohol and gives him some coffee to sober him up. After drinking coffee for the next hour, what is his estimated BAL?

Exercise 2: As part of an organization's initiation ritual, Cindy who weighs 125 pounds is forced to drink screwdrivers containing double shots (1.5 ounce of 80 proof vodka per single shot). She has had seven of these screwdrivers in two hours. Connie has become delirious and her friends place her in a cold shower to sober her up. What is Cindy's estimated BAL after two hours?

Exercise 3: Ralph brings a six pack of average beer with him for a visit with his friends. They are watching a football game on television which lasts four hours. He finished his six pack while watching the game. After leaving his friend's house, he is immediately stopped by the police. He is 20 years old and weighs 180 pounds. Will he get a DUI ticket? If he were 21 years old and weighed 200 pounds would he get a DUI ticket?

Exercise 4: Imagine it is 1 o'clock in the morning and you have had enough alcohol to bring you to a BAL of .18. You decide to stop drinking and go to sleep due to an important 9 o'clock class. What would your estimated BAL be when you entered the class at 9 o'clock in the morning?

Answers to these exercises can be found in the Challenge Results Section at the end of this book.

BAL Chart - Drink/Weight Index

# of drinks	Weight							
	100	120	140	160	180	200	220	240
1 Male	.04	.04	.03	.03	.02	.02	.02	.02
Female	.05	.04	.04	.03	.03	.03	.02	.02
2 Male	.09	.07	.06	.05	.05	.04	.04	.04
Female	.10	.08	.07	.06	.06	.05	.05	.04
3 Male	.13	.11	.09	.08	.07	.07	.06	.05
Female	.15	.13	.11	.10	.08	.08	.07	.06
4 Male	.17	.15	.13	.11	.10	.09	.08	.07
Female	.20	.17	.15	.13	.11	.10	.09	.09
5 Male	.22	.18	.16	.14	.12	.11	.10	.09
Female	.25	.21	.18	.16	.14	.13	.12	.11
6 Male	.26	.22	.19	.16	.15	.13	.12	.11
Female	.30	.26	.22	.19	.17	.15	.14	.13
7 Male	.30	.25	.22	.19	.17	.15	.14	.13
Female	.36	.30	.26	.22	.20	.18	.16	.15
8 Male	.35	.29	.25	.22	.19	.17	.16	.15
Female	.41	.34	.29	.26	.23	.20	.19	.17
9 Male	.39	.33	.28	.25	.22	.20	.18	.16
Female	.46	.38	.33	.29	.26	.23	.21	.19
10 Male	.43	.36	.31	.28	.24	.22	.20	.18
Female	.51	.42	.36	.32	.28	.25	.23	.21
11 Male	.48	.40	.34	.30	.26	.24	.22	.20
Female	.56	.46	.40	.35	.31	.27	.25	.23
12 Male	.53	.43	.37	.32	.29	.26	.24	.21
Female	.61	.50	.43	.37	.33	.30	.28	.25
13 Male	.57	.47	.40	.35	.31	.29	.26	.23
Female	.66	.55	.47	.40	.36	.32	.30	.27
14 Male	.62	.50	.43	.37	.34	.31	.28	.25
Female	.71	.59	.51	.43	.39	.35	.32	.29
15 Male	.66	.54	.47	.40	.36	.34	.30	.27
Female	.76	.63	.55	.46	.42	.37	.35	.32

Remember!!! This is only an *estimation* based on an average metabolic rate. Differences in metabolic rates, gender, types of drinks, food in the stomach etc. can contribute to substantial differences in your Blood Alcohol Levels. Also, there may be slight differences (.01 - .03) between the various BAL Charts that are available to you.

Alcohol

Reflections:

a. How many drinks would it take for you to attain a BAL of .08 after 3 hours? after four hours?

b. Think about the last time you or a friend was impaired. What was the peak BAL during that experience?

b. How can you utilize this formula?

Chapter Three

Drinks

... beer, wine, liquor —

what's the difference?

*"When we actually calculated the percentage of alcohol in differ-
ent drinks it was interesting. It made me think twice about how
much I drink."*

Betty T., Keene State College sophomore

Drinks

I F YOU CHOOSE TO DRINK ALCOHOL, not only is it important that you understand *what* it is you are drinking but also *how much*. Students often arrive at a party and head straight to the keg, the punch bowl or maybe the shot bar. They start drinking whatever is available with no knowledge of what or how much they are drinking. One drink is equal to a half ounce of pure ethyl alcohol which can be "packaged" as a 12-ounce regular beer, a 4-ounce glass of regular table wine, a 1-ounce shot of 100-proof liquor or a 1.5-ounce shot of 80 proof liquor.

If you choose to consume alcohol, be an informed consumer!

Beer

"It's not like I drink the hard stuff. It's only beer."
Jenn M., New Hampshire College first-year student

"Beer is for real men."
John L., University of Maine sophomore

Beer has the reputation of being somewhat less dangerous than other alcoholic beverages. The only difference between the alcohol in beer and that in other beverages is the concentration or volume of alcohol in the drink. The alcohol is the same—ethyl alcohol. Most regular beers contain between 4 percent and 6 percent of alcohol by volume. This means that in an average 12-ounce can of beer there is approximately one-half ounce of alcohol. The rest of the 11 1/2-ounces contain things like Bavarian hops, only the finest barley of course, and perhaps a dash of "Rocky Mountain spring water."
12 ounces regular beer x .045 = .54 ounces of alcohol

Here's the approximate volume of alcohol in a number of beers available across the country:

Amstel Light	3.04
Bass Ale	5.08
Beck's	5.07
Black Label	4.50
Budweiser	4.75
Budweiser Light	3.60
Busch	4.60
Coors	4.75
Coors Light	4.19
Dos Equis	4.75
Killian's Red Ale	5.42
Harley Davidson	5.10
Heineken	5.00
Michelob	4.90
Michelob Light	4.20
Miller	4.86
Miller Light	4.18
Moosehead	4.82
Natural Light	4.20
Pabst Blue Ribbon	4.72
Rolling Rock	4.52
Samuel Adams	4.62
Stroh's	4.50
Whitebread	4.40

The beer industry has developed a product called "ice" beer. Ostensibly, this product is a result of the industry's desire to provide us with a richer flavor. It is interesting to note, however, that this richer flavor comes with an increase in the alco-

MeSorley's Old Ale House is the oldest of the typical pre-Civil War saloons still operating in New York City. It was founded in 1854 and is the only true ale house left in the world. The only liquid refreshment sold is ale. When asked why he never sold anything else (or stronger) such as whiskey, John MeSorley, the founder, explained, "Ale is potent enough for any man."

hol content of the beer— alcohol, the substance that causes addiction. During the early 1980s, beer sales of large U.S. brewers began to decline. The industry counted on the extra kick in ice beer to spark the staggering beer market of the 1990s. Ice beers tend to contain between 5.5 percent and 8 percent of alcohol by volume, approximately 50 percent more alcohol than regular beers.

12 ounces ice beer x .06 = .72 ounces of alcohol

Here's the approximate volume of alcohol in a number of widely available ice beers:

Budweiser Ice Draft 5.48

Labatt's Ice Beer 5.60

Miller Icehouse..5.42

Molson Ice 5.19

Malt liquors also contain more alcohol than regular beer, averaging about 7 percent of alcohol by volume.

12 ounces malt liquor x .07 = .84 ounces of alcohol

Here's the volume of alcohol in a number of common malt liquors:

Colt 45 M. L..5.90

EKU M. L. 10.90

Elephant M. L..7.20

Golden Hawk M. L..6.50

Schlitz M.L. 5.80

If you choose to consume alcohol, be an informed consumer!

Table Wine

"I hate the taste of beer. I'm not too crazy about wine either - but I have to drink something so I sip wine."
Stephanie F., Pennsylvania State University junior

Regular table wines (Beaujolais, Chardonay, Cabernet Sauvignon, Chablis, Rhine, etc.) usually contain approximately 12 percent of alcohol by volume. The volume will never be higher than 14 percent for a simple reason. The fermentation process that produces wine relies on the interaction of the natural sugars of various fruits and grains with either wild yeast in the air or commercial yeast. When a volume of between 12 and 14 percent alcohol is reached in the fermenting juice, fermentive yeast can no longer survive. The production of alcohol then ceases. Therefore, a 4-ounce glass of wine contains around half an ounce of alcohol. The rest of the drink is juice and other additives.

4 ounces regular table wine x .12 = .48 ounces of alcohol

If you choose to consume alcohol, be an informed consumer!

Wine Coolers

"It is a common belief among college students that wine coolers are for women and wimps."

Anonymous

"I had no idea they had that much alcohol! No wonder I got wrecked the other night."

Jenny B., University of Connecticut first-year student

Wine coolers have acquired the reputation of being a "girl's" drink or a "sissy" drink. If you are not an informed consumer, you might believe this. After all, they do seem innocent enough. The fact is, however, that wine coolers contain between 3 percent and 7 percent volume of alcohol with an average volume of approximately 6 percent.

12 ounce average wine cooler x .06 = .72 ounces of alcohol

In other words, many 12-ounce wine coolers could contain almost 50 percent more alcohol than an average 12-ounce beer. Therefore, depending on the brand, a six pack of average beer could be equal to a four pack of average wine coolers!

If you choose to consume alcohol, be an informed consumer!

Fortified Wine

"Man, that stuff is deadly."

Michael V., University of Connecticut junior

Drinks

Some wine companies will fortify or increase the alcohol content of the wine by simply adding more alcohol. The result is called fortified wine. These extra potent wines can contain anywhere from a 14 percent to 24 percent volume of alcohol. A particularly dangerous fortified wine called "Cisco" is available in some states. It's also known on the streets as "liquid crack." Whenever I mention this product in class, I usually hear a number of moans and groans of recognition. Those responses usually come from students who have tried Cisco. Cisco tastes a bit like cough medicine, is cheap, is available in 12-ounce bottles or liters and has a 20 percent volume of alcohol. (A weaker form called Cisco Tropicals has a 14.9 percent volume of alcohol.)

12 ounces of Cisco x .20 = 2.4 ounces of alcohol

So a 12-ounce bottle of Cisco is equal to five drinks. After hearing about this drink, some students half-jokingly inquire, "Where can we get it?" It is illegal in many states because it exceeds the acceptable volume of alcohol for a fortified wine, as established by the respective state liquor authorities. If I, as a 180-pound male, were to drink a 12-ounce bottle of Cisco in one hour, my blood alcohol level would be about .10 percent—legally drunk! A 110-pound female would have a BAL of approximately .23 percent. If she were encouraged to have another shortly after by a friend or her date, her BAL would increase to approximately .44 percent. She would be at high risk for a serious impairment problem!

If you choose to consume alcohol, be an informed consumer!

Liquor

> *"I knew I got drunk faster when I was drinking mixed drinks but I didn't know why."*
>
> Jason M., Keene State College sophomore

The alcohol content of liquor is referred to as "proof." Proof is exactly twice the volume of alcohol. A 100-proof liquor contains a 50 percent volume of alcohol. An 80-proof liquor contains a 40 percent volume of alcohol.

1 ounce of 100-proof vodka x .50 = .50 ounces of alcohol
1.5 ounces of 80-proof whiskey x .40 = .60 ounces of alcohol

Possibly the vilest (from a Western point of view) liquor was yan-yang-tskew, a Chinese rot gut made from fermented sheep's flesh and, in one province, from the fermenting carcasses of plump puppy dogs. "Lamb-wine" was said to be especially strong, a favorite among Tartars and Mongols. Genghis Kahn liked it.

There are some special considerations with regard to drinking liquor. Liquor contains little nutritional value. When we drink liquor, therefore, it is absorbed into our bloodstream very quickly. When I was 18, I enjoyed reading James Bond adventures. And, of course, in an attempt to emulate my hero and impress my date, I once ordered a vodka martini. After just two of these, I felt like I had been hit in the head with a sledgehammer! It seemed as though the vodka went straight into my bloodstream. And, to some degree it did. I was drinking on an empty stomach, and the martini had no food content to slow the absorption. If the vodka had been mixed with some tomato juice, Worcestershire sauce, horseradish, salt and pepper, making a bloody mary, it would have taken a little longer for the vodka to enter my bloodstream because the food content of the juice would have slowed the absorption—but James Bond did not drink bloody marys and I sure embarrassed myself in front of my date after a few martinis. Here is an overview of various amounts of alcohol in some liquors:

Whiskey	80 - 150 proof	40% - 75% volume
Vodka	80 - 100 proof	40% - 50% volume
Gin	80 - 98 proof	40% - 48% volume
Rum	80 - 151 proof	40% - 75% volume
Tequila	90 - 100 proof	45% - 50% volume

Punch

"I was handed a glass of punch. It tasted great so I had a few more and so on. I never tasted any alcohol. All of a sudden it hit me. I was hammered! I had to get 'escorted' home, where I proceeded to vomit and pass out. I never had a worse hangover than that one. Since then, if I don't plan on drinking I bring my own non-alcoholic beverage."

Allison E., Keene State College junior

Drinks

At many parties a wide variety of fruit juice punches are served. These punches are generally spiked with some mild-tasting type of liquor such as vodka. Do not simply assume that one glass of punch will be equal to one drink (half ounce of alcohol) as previously described. Quite often this is not the case because a large quantity of alcohol can be hidden by the sweet-tasting fruit juices. For your own safety and well-being, avoid these spiked punches regardless of how good or "innocent" they may taste. One other reason for avoiding punch is the potential for the addition of other drugs to this dangerous mix. There are now a number of drugs circulating around many campuses, such as Rohypnol or GHB, which can be added to punch as well as other drinks and are undetectable by the drinker. These drugs can cause the drinker to become extremely impaired, helpless, and perhaps cause an extended blackout or even death.

If you choose to consume alcohol, be an informed consumer!   ♦

Personal Challenge: Alcohol Attitudes

Goal:
To assess your attitudes about alcohol.

Instructions:
Circle the words that best describe your feelings about the following sentences.

1. People enjoy being around me more when I've had a few drinks.
STRONGLY AGREE   AGREE   NOT SURE   DISAGREE   STRONGLY DISAGREE

2. I can have a few drinks without my driving being affected.
STRONGLY AGREE   AGREE   NOT SURE   DISAGREE   STRONGLY DISAGREE

3. Alcohol helps me get through stressful situations.
STRONGLY AGREE   AGREE   NOT SURE   DISAGREE   STRONGLY DISAGREE

4. Drinking changes my personality for the worse.
STRONGLY AGREE   AGREE   NOT SURE   DISAGREE   STRONGLY DISAGREE

5. Drinking regularly could result in my becoming addicted to alcohol.
STRONGLY AGREE   AGREE   NOT SURE   DISAGREE   STRONGLY DISAGREE

6. Drinking alcohol is bad for my health.
STRONGLY AGREE   AGREE   NOT SURE   DISAGREE   STRONGLY DISAGREE

7. I could have family problems if I drank everyday.
STRONGLY AGREE   AGREE   NOT SURE   DISAGREE   STRONGLY DISAGREE

8. I have more fun at social events when I drink.
STRONGLY AGREE   AGREE   NOT SURE   DISAGREE   STRONGLY DISAGREE

9. Alcohol has been a negative influence on my life.
STRONGLY AGREE   AGREE   NOT SURE   DISAGREE   STRONGLY DISAGREE

10. My friendships would be damaged if I drank a lot.
STRONGLY AGREE   AGREE   NOT SURE   DISAGREE   STRONGLY DISAGREE

11. I feel more confident when I drink alcohol.
STRONGLY AGREE   AGREE   NOT SURE   DISAGREE   STRONGLY DISAGREE

Drinks

12. Drinking alcohol is a good way for me to relax and loosen up.
STRONGLY AGREE   AGREE   NOT SURE   DISAGREE   STRONGLY DISAGREE

13. I would feel ashamed if I drank too much.
STRONGLY AGREE   AGREE   NOT SURE   DISAGREE   STRONGLY DISAGREE

14. I would have problems at school if I drank more than I do now.
STRONGLY AGREE   AGREE   NOT SURE   DISAGREE   STRONGLY DISAGREE

15. I would have lower grades if I drank more than I do now.
STRONGLY AGREE   AGREE   NOT SURE   DISAGREE   STRONGLY DISAGREE

16. Drinking is a good way to forget my problems.
STRONGLY AGREE   AGREE   NOT SURE   DISAGREE   STRONGLY DISAGREE

17. It is okay if I get drunk once in awhile.
STRONGLY AGREE   AGREE   NOT SURE   DISAGREE   STRONGLY DISAGREE

18. I feel that driving a car after having a few drinks is a stupid thing to do.
STRONGLY AGREE   AGREE   NOT SURE   DISAGREE   STRONGLY DISAGREE

19. I would feel more popular if I drank alcohol.
STRONGLY AGREE   AGREE   NOT SURE   DISAGREE   STRONGLY DISAGREE

20. Drinking alcohol is a normal part of the college experience.
STRONGLY AGREE   AGREE   NOT SURE   DISAGREE   STRONGLY DISAGREE

Answers to these exercises can be found in the Challenge Results Section at the end of this book..

Reflections:

After completing the survey, ask yourself the following questions:
a. How do you feel about the results of this survey?
b. Review your answers and score on each individual question. How do you feel about your scores on each of these attitudes?
c. What role does alcohol play in your life?

Adapted from Program Evaluation Handbook: Alcohol Abuse Education (1988). Center for Disease Control and the Office of Disease Prevention and Health Promotion, U.S. Department of Health and Human Services.

Chapter Four

Risks

... so what's the big deal?

"I heard recently that alcohol makes students think they are ten feet tall and bullet proof. I contend that as many students get older, alcohol chops them 'down to size' and that some of their perspectives are 'shot full of holes'."

Kristina D., Manhattan College senior

"I often see students making choices without first thinking about the consequences. They do not seem to have the strength to withstand their immediate impulses. They need to develop the skills to look beyond the immediate gratification."

Charlie J., SUNY Cortland senior

"Many people drink to become more social but end up incoherent. Many people drink to diminish their problems but only see them multiply. Many people drink to be the life of the party and end up being the fool. Many people drink to make themselves feel better but wake up feeling worse. Many people drink to add pleasure to their lives but only end up hurting themselves and others."

Christina D., Keene State College junior

Risks

W E ALL WOULD LIKE TO HAVE OUR CAKE and eat it too—and not gain weight either! Those of us who drink would love to enjoy the pleasures alcohol can provide but not face the risks inherent in getting impaired. The reality is, however, that as we drink and increase our level of impairment, we increase our risk for impairment problems. The more often we get impaired the more often we risk experiencing impairment problems.

Numerous research projects conducted around the country support the premise that most students do not consume alcohol at a high risk level. For instance, the results of the 1998 Core Survey,[5] a statistically reliable and valid research instrument administered on more than 60 campuses to over 30,000 randomly selected students across the country, indicate that approximately 56 percent of students either don't drink or average one drink per week. Another 21 percent average between two and five drinks per week. Even though most college students are not experiencing alcohol problems, there is a high profile minority of students who consume at a high risk level which results in a number of problems for them. Here are just some of those problems:

- 63 percent had at least one hangover, 45 percent had at least two hangovers, and 34 percent had three or more hangovers
- 53 percent reported vomiting after drinking
- 33 percent missed a class due to drinking
- 34 percent reported driving while under the influence of alcohol
- 30 percent got into a fight or an argument while drinking
- 12 percent reported having been taken advantage of sexually while under the influence of alcohol
- 31 percent reported having a memory loss (blackout).

Between 1987 and 1992 the number of emergency room admissions for alcohol poisoning in campus communities jumped 15 percent. At one school, cases of alcohol poisoning doubled during the same time period.[6] Regrettably, there's not much evidence indicating a significant decrease in these problems today.

It is important to emphasize once again that although these statistics indicate that drinking is taking a serious toll on many students, most students are not experiencing these problems on a regular basis. Since most students do not drink at a high risk level then most students do not experience blackouts, most students do not miss class due to drinking, most students do not drive under the influence of alcohol and most students do not experience more than two hangovers in a year. It is a minority of students who are drinking heavily and not only experiencing these problems but also disrupting the lives of students who are making healthier choices. These heavy drinkers also intrude on the safe environment desired by the majority of students. Later you will see why it is important for you to get involved in campus alcohol and other drug education and abuse prevention efforts.

I hear many students claim, "When I get out in the real world, I'll cut back on my drinking." It scares me to hear so many students deluding themselves. The college campus does not have a protective dome surrounding it. Campus hangovers are just as painful and debilitating as off-campus hangovers, the rapes that occur on campus are no less traumatic than street rapes, the AIDS contracted on campus is just as deadly as that contracted off-campus. Granted, campus life is different from the so-called work world. *But, the campus is the real world.* There are different responsibilities and stresses, but it is real the real world. Don't let your professors or college administrators, or your peers for that matter, minimize your college life by referring to it as somehow less than real.

Blackouts

"My mind became as dark as the night. I was at the party and the next thing I was back in my dorm—in the girls' bathroom no less—throwing up. That's all I remember. I'm not quite sure what happened between the party and then back in the dorm."
Mike L., Plymouth State College sophomore

"At breakfast my friends laughed at me when they first saw me. Then they told me about what a fool I had made of myself. I didn't remember any of it."
Chris C., University of Massachusetts sophomore

Risks

"I can remember when I experienced a blackout after a long afternoon of drinking. Apparently I made a blatant remark about a girl's physical features and she was embarrassed and upset. I had no recollection of it until her friends told me about it. I was so disappointed in myself. I couldn't believe a remark like that could come out of my mouth. I eventually apologized for my behavior."

Raphael D., Boston University junior

A blackout is a form of alcohol-induced amnesia. Do not confuse this with passing out or fainting. While it is happening, the drinker is conscious but unaware that he or she is in a blackout. Although obviously impaired, the drinker appears to function ordinarily, but after sobering up cannot recall some of the people or events from the night before. It's usually not until the next day when the previous night's "war stories" are being shared in the dining hall that the drinker realizes a blackout occurred.

It has been difficult to research this phenomenon because we don't know when or how someone enters a blackout. Apparently, the neurotransmitters in the brain responsible for maintaining memories for some reason cease functioning. We don't know how much or how often a person needs to drink in order to experience a blackout. However, we do know that most, but not all, alcoholics have experienced blackouts. More importantly, we know that you do not need to be an alcoholic to experience a blackout. A blackout places you at risk for a serious impairment problem and indicates that a serious alcohol problem has developed or is developing.

One other point regarding blackouts, many people mistakenly say "I never get so wasted that I have a blackout." You do not need to be "totally wasted" in order to experience a blackout. Slight impairment alone can contribute to a blackout.

Hangovers

"I was always getting loaded. I'd get up the next day and drink a beer to cure the hangover."

Anonymous

"I get up around noon. I usually take four Advil. Then I struggle over to the dining hall. Some of the people there look like they were in a train wreck. I can't believe we're all doing this to our bodies."

Dennis D., Keene State College sophomore

"This year I've stuck with my two drink limit. I have a better time at parties, I'm not hungover, I remember who I met the night before and my grades have gotten much, much better."

Wendy R., Plymouth State College senior

The Germans call it "wailing of cats" *(Katzenjammer)*, the Italians "out of tune" *(stonato)*, the French "woody mouth" *(Gueule de bois)*, the Norwegians "workmen in my head" *(jeg har tommermenn)* and the Swedes call it—my favorite—"pain in the roots of my hair" *(hont i haret)*.[7] If you have experienced a hangover, I'm sure you can relate to any or all of these descriptions of a hangover.

Basically, a hangover is the body's way of telling us we have had too much to drink. Alcohol not only irritates the digestive system, it also dehydrates the body. It is important to rehydrate after a night of alcohol consumption. Be careful though, there is evidence that rehydrating too quickly can actually worsen the headache due to the erratic changes in body fluids. Congeners, the by-product of the fermentation process, also contribute to hangovers. Although alcohol is eliminated from the body at an average rate of one-half ounce per hour, the congeners take much longer. These substances provide the unique flavor to various alcoholic beverages,

Mike Finn was a famous flat boat man and whiskey guzzler. He was once engaged in a shooting match in which he and his rival competed in shooting full whiskey glasses from the top of each other's head. Finn missed intentionally and shot the other man dead, paying off an old grudge, some say. Finn was the subject of many whiskey legends. He is said to have swallowed a whole buffalo robe with its hair on to serve as a new stomach lining, his old, original one having been destroyed by drinking oceans of Monongahela rye.

but they are toxic. If you drink, when considering what type of alcoholic beverage to consume and the hangover potential, keep in mind that vodka and gin are low in congener content, blended scotch has about four times the amount of congeners as vodka and gin, while brandy, rum and pure malt scotch have six times more. Bourbon contains approximately thirty times the amount of congeners than vodka.

There are no real "cures" for a hangover. So-called cures simply relieve only some of the discomfort and stress of the painful symptoms of the hangover. Even so, there are many bizarre suggestions for curing a hangover. Voodoo legend suggests that you stick pins into the cork of the bottle from which you drank. The Norwegians drink a glass of heavy cream, the Russians prefer salted cucumber juice, and the Swiss use brandy with peppermint. In one way, none of these work, and in another, all of them do. The reason: The most powerful hangover remedy is belief in the curative value of whatever you do, whether it is steaming in a sauna or sticking your head in a freezer.[8] Physiologically, however, we find that none of these actually "cure" the hangover.

By the way, *do not* mix alcohol with aspirin, ibuprofen or other anti-inflammatory drugs. This combination can cause serious damage to your stomach. Also *do not* mix alcohol with acetaminophen, the medicine found in Tylenol. This combination can cause serious damage to your liver.

I'm sure you've noticed that people experiencing a hangover tend to be anxious and on edge. Some students have learned they can relieve this anxiety by having a little "hair of the dog that bit you." This means curing your hangover by taking a drink of whatever it was that caused it.

"A little hair of the dog" may seem like a viable solution, and here's why. Picture yourself standing in a pool of water that is about chest high. Hold a ball in your hands, depress it underwater, then release it; it will rebound above the waterline. Depress it even further and it rebounds further. It's the same with alcohol and the central nervous system. If I depress my central nervous system with the depressant drug alcohol and then stop, it will rebound—not back to normal, but to a level of high anxiety. What can I do to relieve this anxiety? Have a drink of the depressant—alcohol. We should, however, be very clear about this: Drinking to cure a hangover is an indication that alcohol has become or is becoming a problem in your life.

Why don't we recognize the use of "a little hair of the dog" as problematic behavior? Probably because society, and in particular the alcohol and restaurant industries, have normalized this addictive activity. Champagne breakfasts and brunches, complete with champagne and many other drinks like bloody marys, screwdrivers, and mimosas, are considered socially acceptable—even though they encourage the development of addictive behavior patterns.

Alcohol Poisoning

> *"At first we didn't want to call the hospital but we could hardly feel her pulse. Later the doctor told us that she was very close to dying."*
>
> Jessica S., Keene State College junior

> *"He was my best friend and now he's gone. Damn it. I wish I would have done something to prevent it."*
>
> Anonymous

One serious concern about alcohol consumption which sometimes falls through the cracks when it comes to alcohol education and abuse prevention, is the reality that heavy alcohol consumption can kill. This is not meant as a scare tactic however, death due to heavy alcohol consumption is a reality. It is a tragic reality that hits students and their families and friends too often, every semester, throughout the country. Just a few of these tragedies include a student who, in 1996, after attending a couple of parties, had a BAL of .31 percent and died of alcohol poisoning. That same year, another student died of alcohol poisoning after drinking six beers and twelve shots during a two hour period and developing a BAL of .34 percent. In 1997 a student died of alcohol poisoning after an initiation activity which included chugging exorbitant amounts of alcohol resulting in a BAL of .48 percent. As part of a twenty first birthday celebration in 1998 a student died of alcohol poisoning after consuming 24 shots during a three hour period resulting in a BAL of more than .45 percent. These are just a few examples of how dangerous high risk drinking can be.

Symposium is the Greek term for "drinking together." At a symposium the guests elected a leader who decided whether to drink the wine neat or mixed, whether to drink little or much.

Risks

Alcohol is a depressant drug. When large volumes are consumed in a short period of time, such as when chugging or participating in drinking games, it can depress the central nervous system so much that the messages from the autonomic nervous system that control your basic survival functions—heartbeat and breathing—slow down, sometimes so slow we stop breathing and our heart stops beating.

How much alcohol does it take to kill someone? The answer varies with each individual and with different circumstances. As you can see by the tragedies described previously, some people can die from a BAL of .31 percent while others can consume more alcohol before reaching a deadly BAL. We know that a BAL of .25 percent and above puts us at much greater risk for falls, traffic crashes, asphyxiation from choking while vomiting and other serious incidents. The risk for death from alcohol poisoning starts around here too. The higher the BAL the greater the risk for death due to alcohol poisoning. At .30 percent you may pass out. The BAL which would cause someone to pass out is dangerously close to a deadly BAL. At .35 percent you could stop breathing and at .40 percent you could fall into a coma, cause possible brain damage and be more likely to die from alcohol poisoning.

> *"The doctors told us that if we waited any longer our friend could have died"*
>
> Jenn A., Penn State University junior

Helping an intoxicated person

Here are some tips to consider when dealing with an intoxicated person:
- if the person is vomiting have her/him either sit up or lay on his/her side in the fetal position to avoid choking.
- if the person has cold, clammy, pale or bluish skin, call medical personnel immediately.
- passing out is a sign of a potentially serious situation. If you can't wake up the person, either call 911, your college emergency service or get them to the hospital. Do not assume the drinker will simply sleep it off.
- in cases where there is erratic breathing (less than 8 breaths per minute or more than 10 seconds between breaths) get to the emergency room immediately.
- in the meantime, do not give the drinker, coffee, liquids, food, or a cold shower. Also do not force the person to exercise.
- if in doubt, get assistance immediately. While seeking assistance, if possible, try to have someone stay with the drinker. This can be a life and death situation.

One of the primary reasons students do not seek help for their friends who may be at risk for deadly, acute alcohol poisoning is they are afraid the drinker will get in trouble with college officials or the police. Please keep in mind, the minor inconvenience of dealing with some later campus judicial action is nothing compared to the pain of the tragedy you may prevent. By reporting your concern about the intoxication level of your friend or acquaintance to the police, medical personnel or college officials you could save his/her life.

Academics

"I now realize that freshman year I was making some really high risk choices. When I think back to my three nights per week— drunken stupors—I'm horrified. I cannot believe I had no clue as to the damage I was inflicting on my body. My grades suffered, I nearly got arrested and I gained twenty five pounds. I even altered my schedule to accommodate my drinking. It scares me to think I did this. Now, because I've cut back drastically on my drinking, my grades have significantly improved, my attitude is health oriented and I completely lost my beer weight."

Yvonne J., Franklin Pierce College junior

"I know some people who have been here five or six years and still drink every weekend for entertainment. I think this is why they've been in school so long."

Joe U., University of Florida senior

"I was drinking big time. I received a 1.5 that semester and to top it off I got arrested and had to pay about three hundred dollars worth of fines."

Seth J., Manhattan College junior

"My Dad always told me to profit from others' mistakes. But, I needed to learn myself. And it cost me. My freshman year is just a big blur. Academically I—shall we say—was not fully engaged. It took me a couple of years of lousy GPAs to learn what was more important—partying or good grades."

Carla A., Pennsylvania State University senior

Risks

"I used to party throughout the week. After my freshman year I cut down. I'm lucky I didn't get kicked out. My GPA was 1.4 but the forgiveness policy helped me get it up to a 2.0. What a shock. I was an honor roll student in high school."

Mike M., Keene State College senior

"Thursday, Friday and Saturday nights were all I looked forward to. School work wasn't even at the bottom of my list."

Cindy V., Keene State College junior

Alcohol is implicated in more than 40 percent of all academic problems and 28 percent of all dropouts.[9] Research indicates that, on average, college students who drink the most alcohol earn the lowest grades. Students with D or F grade point averages report consuming an average of 10 drinks weekly, C students average 8 drinks weekly, B students average 6 drinks per week and A students average 4 drinks per week.[10] Yes there are students who can "party hard" and still maintain an A average, but they are the exception to the rule. Most students who drink at a high risk level experience academic problems.

Alcohol consumption can affect your grade point average for a number of reasons. High risk drinkers miss more classes due to their drinking. After all, it's quite difficult to sit through an hour-and-a-half lecture while dealing with a severe hangover. National research indicates that 21 percent of students who binge drank* had fallen behind in their schoolwork and 30 percent had missed class because of their drinking since the beginning of the school year. Among frequent binge drinkers, students who had binged three or more times in two weeks prior to the survey, 46 percent had fallen behind in schoolwork and 60 percent had missed class because of their drinking. Only a fraction of non-binge drinkers fell behind in their studies or missed class because of drinking (6 percent and 8 percent, respectively).[11] I suspect many high risk drinkers also submit projects late due to their lifestyle choices. It's difficult to keep up with schoolwork when your primary concern is which party will have the most kegs.

---

* A "binge" is defined by researchers as five or more drinks in one sitting for men and four or more drinks in one sitting for women. One of the problems with this definition is that it does not take into account the period of time during which the drinking took place. For the purposes of this book, whenever referring to a "binge" it will refer to the aforementioned definition. Both the definition of "binge" as well as the use of the term have been called into question by many alcohol education and abuse prevention specialists and certainly deserves further analysis.

Finally, and most important, many students believe that as long as they don't drink the night before an exam, alcohol consumption will have no impact on their test-taking ability. This couldn't be further from the truth. Here's why: our brains are made up of millions of nerve cells that transmit messages through an intricate series of chemical and electrical impulses. The sensitive chemical balance necessary to keep this neurological network operating is disrupted by the presence of alcohol. And this chemical imbalance caused by the alcohol remains even after the alcohol is metabolized. Research indicates that this chemical imbalance can last for up to thirty days after the alcohol has been metabolized—even when a person is completely sober.[12] This imbalance impairs our abstract thinking skills. Those are the skills needed to bring two separate thoughts together in order to develop a third concept. So, the bottom line is drinking can possibly impair our abstract thinking skills, resulting in impaired test-taking ability, even thirty days after consuming alcohol.

Driving Under the Influence

"One instant can change your life. It can impact your life FOR-EVER. The person must deal with the consequences for the rest of his or her life."

Jennifer S., Boston University first-year student

"I realized while watching the DUI video that my friends and I have not only risked our own lives but also other peoples' lives too."

Anonymous

"I rationalized a near fatal car accident at age 18 on excessive speed not alcohol."

Anonymous

"I have fought with so many drunk people. It's so frustrating. They don't see that you're trying to help—not ruin their 'good time'."

Cheryl C., New England College senior

"Then my sister got a DUI. My mother was real disappointed. How can my mother contradict herself like that? She says 'It's OK for her to drink and drive because she's older and has a lot

more experience.' How can you be an experienced drunk driver?"

Anonymous

"My friends and I have gone out and had some drinks and we drove to and from the locations. We would make sure whoever was driving would not drink a lot and that they were OK to drive."

John Z., Massachusetts Institute of Technology junior

"I always keep a reserve of ten dollars in my shoe when I go out on a date. Just in case he drinks when he is driving I can get a cab home."

Anonymous

"My friends and I are going to have to do a lot of changing when it comes to drinking and driving. We are going to have a real designated driver, one who does not drink at all. Or, we will take public transportation."

Jeff Z., Massachusetts Institute of Technology sophomore

During the time it takes you to read this book, approximately ten people will die (approximately one every twenty-thirty minutes) due to an alcohol-related car crash. And, chances are that many of these victims will be college students. In spite of all the educational programs now being conducted, all the prevention programs now implemented, all the increased enforcement of DUI laws, more than 30 percent of our college students still report driving while under the influence of alcohol.[13] In 1995, sixteen to twenty four year olds accounted for 40% of fatal alcohol related highway crashes. And, alcohol related crashes are still the number one cause of death for sixteen to twenty four year olds.[14]

The designated driver program has undoubtedly saved many lives. But, as indicated in the above statistics, the designated driver program seems to have lost some of its impact. Perhaps one reason for this is that on the college campus, a dangerous new practice is basing the selection of the designated driver on the one who drank the least! And, look who's deciding who's the least drunk—all the drunks. How can they judge? If you are the designated driver, don't drink. If you have decided to use a designated driver, do not get into the car if that person has had even just a few drinks. It's not worth the risk. Choose a safer alternative... take a cab, call a friend, walk, or even stay at the party.

Contrary to what many high risk drinkers would like to believe, you do not drive better while under the influence of alcohol. You may think you do, because you know you take extra care while driving. But your perception of your driving performance is also impaired. Research indicates that the greater your impairment, the higher your risk of an impairment problem, especially the problem of an alcohol-related car crash.[15]

What more can be said about this continuing problem? The education and prevention programs are working only minimally. One of the difficulties is that when you need to make one of the most important decisions of your life—to drive or not—you may never be less capable of making that decision if you are under the influence of alcohol. Also, keep in mind, the choice to have a designated driver is not a license to drink uncontrollably. Using a designated driver will lower your risk for an alcohol related car crash but will not lower your risk for the numerous other dangers associated with high risk drinking.

Sex

"Although people say they are aware of how you get AIDS, and they say they are scared, it's amazing that they seem not to think about it when they are drinking. They're out drinking and having a good time—then they have sex with someone they don't even know."

Jennifer T., Rivier College senior

"Doesn't it scare them with so many STDs in the world. How can people risk their lives for one night of enjoyment? I don't know how many times I've heard my friends talk about one night stands and then they just laugh about it. How can you laugh about something that could take your life? And, of course, all these one night stands are alcohol related."

Ryan A., Keene State College senior

"I'm afraid my friends are going to learn the hard way."

Jess T., Pennsylvania State University sophomore

"Personally, I have always worn a condom but I did not necessarily care about who I was sleeping with."

Anonymous

Risks

"I know a few girls that have gone to have themselves tested. I was shocked."

Anonymous

"It's sad to see a young girl right out of high school fall into the trap. The young freshmen come to school not knowing anyone and it's usually their first time away from home. They meet some guy that's more than happy to keep pouring beer into them. These girls think the guy is just being nice or he likes them. Maybe. Then at the end of the night you see 'Daddy's little girl' stumbling home in the arms of a satisfied predator carrying his prey."

Mike M., Keene State College sophomore

"It's quite scary because you never know when someone you know will have AIDS or maybe even yourself. And when you're drunk, the last thing you think about is safe sex."

Anonymous

"During my sophomore year I went to a party and I had never had a real drink before. Sure my parents gave me a sip of wine here and there but it was my first REAL PARTY. You know what I mean. My friends started handing me bottles of Southern Comfort. Soon I was loaded. I couldn't even see. Well, to make matters worse that was the night I lost my virginity and I don't even remember it. Yes, every female's worst nightmare."

Anonymous

"The thing I hate to see the most is a drunk female throwing herself at some guy. And people wonder how date rapes happen—not that I am blaming the females. It just gets so confusing when booze is involved."

Chris T., Plymouth State College junior

If we were to believe all the statements and images presented by the alcohol advertising industry, we would view alcohol as a necessity for a successful, pleasurable sex life. Some people do believe that alcohol increases your sexual desire and improves your performance. But, physiologically speaking, alcohol has the opposite effect. Research strongly indicates that alcohol contributes to sexual dysfunction in men.

As Shakespeare noted in the tragedy *Macbeth*, alcohol "provokes the desire, but it takes away the performance." In one study, the ability of college men to achieve an erection while watching erotic films was impaired at blood alcohol levels below the legal intoxication point.[16] In much the same way, alcohol decreases the sexual pleasure of women. This is due to the fact that alcohol reduces vaginal vasocongestion during sexual activity. The conclusions of this research are inescapable: Alcohol negatively affects the ability to perform and/or enjoy sexual activity.

Just like music and lighting, alcohol may enhance or establish a romantic mood. But, due to its disinhibiting action, high risk alcohol consumption also contributes to increased sexual promiscuity on our campuses today. Between 35-70 percent of college students report engaging in some type of sexual activity primarily as a result of alcohol. For example, at Dartmouth, 46 percent of students admit that, while under the influence of alcohol, they had sex they would not have engaged in had they been sober.[17] And, nearly one out of five students report abandoning safer sex practices while under the influence of alcohol.[18] Students engaging in unplanned sexual encounters as a result of alcohol consumption risk a number of assorted problems ranging from embarrassment, guilt, and other emotional difficulties to pregnancy and sexually transmitted disease (STD)—including, of course, AIDS. Sixty percent of college women surveyed who had acquired sexually transmitted diseases, including AIDS and genital herpes, reported being under the influence of alcohol at the time they had intercourse.[19]

Combining alcohol and sexual activity could be a recipe for a disaster. Sexually transmitted diseases can have a dramatic impact on the lives of the victims. If you want to avoid an STD, the safest way, obviously, is abstinence. Abstinence will also help you avoid many of the other challenges associated with such an intimate experience. However, if we consume alcohol, one of the first things impaired is our judgment. It relaxes us and has the potential to cloud our judgment, especially when it comes to sexual activity. When under the influence, we are more likely to take risks, such as having sex and having it unprotected.

If you are sexually active, (and by the way, based on my own interviews with many students around the country, I have found that most college students are not sexually active on a regular basis) there are some precautions you can take. First of all, talk to potential sexual partners about past sexual history and their use of protection. This is particularly difficult when under the influence of alcohol, so having this conversation while sober is important. Second, have a plan on how to protect yourself (latex condoms, limiting the type of sexual activity, etc.) and stick to it.

Risks

Third, having only one sexual partner without an STD is also lower risk. Fourth, do not use intravenous drugs or if you do, do not share needles.

State Dependent Learning

"We usually do shots before the party. You know, it kinda takes the edge off and makes me more sociable."

Tina L., University of Delaware first-year student

"To most people, drinking alcohol gives them the confidence to be more friendly and out-going."

Johnson T., James Madison University senior

"Nine times out of ten my boyfriend was impaired when he spent the night. The first time he told me he loved me he was drunk. He could never say it to me when he was sober. It took me about four months but I finally got a clue and dumped him."

Anonymous

"I like that 'three beer socially happy' mood."

Anonymous

"All it takes is self-confidence. If you believe in yourself and your friends, you don't need a few beers before you dance. If you are self-confident you will be able to do the same things sober as if you had been drinking. And, just think, you'll be able to remember how much fun you had instead of other people telling you how much fun you had."

Adam C., North Carolina State University senior

Research conducted at Mississippi State University indicates that one of the five primary drinking factors for college students is "relational"—that is, they report drinking helps them to meet and socialize with others.[20] This is not surprising. As teens we often feel insecure and sometimes our inhibitions make it difficult to socialize. This difficulty is a normal part of human development. Teens learn that the depressant effect of alcohol lowers their inhibitions thereby increasing their willingness to interact and socialize with others. Consequently, many students then develop a reliance upon alcohol to help them socialize while in high school or during their college years. State dependent learning refers to the *reliance* on alcohol to help them socialize that eventually develops. There's a problem here, though. The social skills developed while impaired do not transfer very effectively into the sober state. Therefore, the difficulty with socializing while sober continues. The more we socialize while under the influence of alcohol, the more we rely on alcohol to assist us in this socialization. This reliance can continue through college life and beyond.

Some of the students who took the challenge to abstain from alcohol at parties (described in the "Party Time" chapter), experienced and described first hand their own state dependency. Here are some examples:

> "I felt a little uncomfortable because I wasn't used to being sober at a party. Usually when I drink at a party I become a lot more outgoing than I usually would be. When I become intoxicated I find myself talking to people I normally wouldn't talk to or even find myself dancing and other things I wouldn't normally do."

> "We did have a good time but we felt we would have had more fun if we had some beer. Maybe not to get overly drunk but to get us in that 'three beer socially happy' mode. I was talking to this other girl who was a bit tipsy. She was in one of my classes. When we were in class the next day she said hello but was nowhere near as friendly as the night before."

> "I was not feeling quite as friendly as the rest of the people. After a few drinks I would normally talk to people I hardly knew or even carry on conversations with strangers. To be honest, without any alcohol in me I did not talk to anyone but the people I came with."

> "My friends were amazed to find out I was not the Dancing Queen I usually am. Our favorite songs were blaring all night long but when my friends began to dance and urged me to follow, I quickly declined. I felt very self conscious."

Alcohol assists people in meeting others, engaging in sex without inhibitions or guilt and escaping the necessity of working through a relationship.[21] Most studies identify the relaxing of inhibitions in sexual encounters as a primary reason for drinking heavily. However, alcohol also has the potential to interfere with one's ability to be intimate, both physically and emotionally. Although it may initially enhance communication between two people, a resulting relationship may become state dependent. If you have chosen to become intimate with another person, monitor your reliance on alcohol as part of your relationship. If alcohol seems to be essential for intimacy, then you are missing out on a truly intimate relationship.

If you do consume alcohol, it is important to monitor its involvement in your social life. Get out and meet people in other circumstances. The final chapter in this book, "Success" describes some interesting alternatives to parties for meeting people.

> **John Wilkes Booth is said to have drunk heavily in a saloon before going to Ford's Theatre to assassinate President Lincoln.**

Violence

"My roommate came home at three in the morning, banging on the door to be let in. She was out with a guy and they both were drinking. He was being rough with her and she fell running away from him. She had split her hand open and it was bleeding everywhere. The next day she went to the doctor and she ended up with a broken hand."

Anonymous

"My roommate came home after a party one night with bruises on her back from some guy."

Anonymous

"I witnessed three fights at a party this weekend. One of the fights was between two girls that were so drunk they could hardly even stand, much less fight. The second fight was between a guy and his girlfriend. He threw her up against the wall. The third fight was between a guy and the guy who threw his girlfriend up against the wall."

Anonymous

Violence erupts on the campus in many ways: residence hall confrontations, bar room brawls, party fights, acquaintance rapes and hate crimes are just a few examples. All tend to have one thing in common, high risk alcohol consumption:

- In a study of dating violence, 25 percent of the college men surveyed admitted to slapping, pushing, or restraining a female partner.[22]
- Several studies estimate that between 50 percent and 80 percent of violence on campus is alcohol related.[23] As a matter of fact, The Campus Violence Prevention Center, a research center at Towson State College, reports that alcohol is a factor in up to 90 percent of violent campus crime.[24]
- One study of residence halls found that 71 percent of violent incidents directed toward resident advisers was alcohol related.[25]
- Alcohol is involved in 80 percent of campus vandalism.[26]
- A study of college men in New England found that binge drinkers were four times as likely as other men to be involved in physical fights.[27]
- The Anti-Defamation League has documented more than 100 incidents of campus anti-Semitic harassment and violence annually between 1991 and 1994 .[28]
- At Yale University and on campuses around the country, approximately 42% of gay and lesbian students experienced some form of physical aggression while on the campus.[29]

Many people believe that campus violence is caused by outsiders entering the campus thereby impacting the campus environment. However, 70 percent of violent campus crime is perpetrated by students and not outsiders.[30]

The question researchers continue to ask is "Why?" Is there something biochemical that creates violent tendencies? Do we, as human beings, have an inherent violent nature that is triggered by alcohol? Or, is it simply the disinhibiting effects of alcohol that cause us to do things our natural social conscience usually prevents us from doing?

Regardless of the reason, we know that alcohol consumption is often associated with violence. If your drinking tends to result in aggression or violent acts, then reevaluate the role alcohol is playing in your life. Is the risk of serious physical harm to you or someone else worth the fleeting pleasures of alcohol consumption? The same is true for your friends and/or special relationships. Is violence a usual result of an evening of drinking with them? If it is, then discuss it with them. If it continues, reevaluate the importance of that friendship or relationship.

Risks

Legal Risks

"Our fraternity lost the lawsuit, It seems like we will be paying forever."

Anonymous

"I was thrown out of the residence halls and then suspended from the college. I am taking classes at night now so I can get back in good standing with the college.

Anonymous

The risk of running into trouble with the law increases significantly when a student engages in high risk drinking. There have been laws regarding alcohol on the books for some time. For example, it has been illegal to consume alcohol if someone is underage. It is illegal to sell alcoholic beverages to someone who is underage. Also, disorderly conduct arising from intoxication has traditionally been considered a legal offense as well. However, historically the law has regarded college life as somewhat distinct from mainstream community life and has carved a "de facto" free space for high risk drinking. It is not that the law condoned high risk drinking, it is simply that the law functioned to overlook many of the problems associated with high risk drinking. In many ways the law showed a prominent symptom, of alcoholism—the law was in denial about the real issues associated with high- risk alcohol use on college campuses.

In recent times the law has changed dramatically. Courts and prosecutors now view high risk alcohol use by college students as a prominent problem. Thus, students now face increased risks of running afoul of the law if they engage in high risk drinking. These risks include:
- criminal prosecution for various alcohol related crimes including disorderly conduct, DUI, use of a false identification, serving or facilitating the use of alcohol by a minor, etc.;
- discipline in the college judicial systems;
- loss of opportunities to sue people who cause injury to a student because the victim was under the influence of alcohol at the time of the injury;
- civil liability for injuries arising from high risk alcohol use;
- notification of a student's alcohol use to parents and other parties;
- loss of opportunities in professional schools and legal problems with professional boards that offer certification in fields such as law, medicine and accounting;
- loss of licenses or the inability to obtain state licenses.

To give you some idea about how serious the law has gotten about high risk drinking on college campuses, it is worth looking at a couple of prominent situations that developed in the 1990s and have serious implications for the future. A first year student at Massachusetts Institute of Technology died of an overdose of alcohol. The students who furnished the alcohol to the first year student - who was underage - were pursued by criminal authorities. In other cases, students who supplied alcohol to fraternity brothers were held civilly responsible for injuries to other students. Florida has recently enacted a law which does not permit a student who has been injured to recover anything if that student was heavily involved in alcohol use. Also, parents may be held responsible for their college-aged student's activities: this can arise through the use of a family automobile and in some cases, states now have laws which penalize parents who provide spaces for underage students to consume alcoholic beverages unlawfully.*

In the generations that preceded, there was an unspoken "right" to drink on campus. Today, like it or not, the law has changed its attitudes and a student who engages in high risk drinking is much more likely to encounter the law in a negative way with long lasting, perhaps damaging future consequences.[31]

Responsible Party Hosting

As the host of a party you can be responsible to your guests by helping them minimize their risk for the problems listed in this chapter. In so doing you will also be minimizing your legal responsibility for the injuries or damages that might occur as a result of your guests' drinking. You can have a wonderful time hosting a party as well as minimize the risk of alcohol related problems for your guests, and in turn for yourself, by following a few responsible hosting tips:

- Arrange for reliable sober monitors that can watch out for guests who may be consuming at a high risk level. They can also help diffuse potentially dangerous situations that may arise.

- Collect car keys when guests arrive. This necessitates that guests get a second

* Special thanks to Peter Lake for his contribution to this section: see generally, Robert D. Bickel and Peter F. Lake, The Rights and Responsibilities of the Modern University: Who Assumes the Risks Of College Life? (Carolina Academic Press: 1999) Stetson College of Law 1401 61st Street South St. Petersburg, FL 33707 727-562-7800

opinion on whether they are sober enough to drive. Promote the use of designated drivers and be prepared to arrange for taxi rides or public transportation.

- Stop serving alcohol an hour before the party ends. As the party draws to a close, provide coffee and food. Remember however, coffee and/or a cold shower does not sober up anyone, it simply wakes them up. Only time allows someone to sober up.

- Mix and serve the drinks yourself or designate a bartender instead of having an open bar. Avoid serving doubles. Use standard measures when mixing drinks.

- If serving an alcoholic punch, use a non-carbonated beverage such as fruit juice as a mixer.

- Always serve food. Cheese, meats, veggies, breads and light dips taste great and don't increase thirst. (Pretzels, popcorn, potato chips etc. are salty and cause people to drink more.)

- Do not encourage or force people to drink. Discourage drinking games.

- Always provide low alcohol and alcohol free drinks such as coffee, soda, fruit juices, and water.

- Avoid games, etc. that involve physical activity because guests who are drinking are more prone to accidents and injuries.   ♦

Personal Challenge: Opportunities

Goal:

To identify the opportunities available to you both academically and socially while on the college campus.

Instructions:

1. Picture yourself as a graduating senior. List your answers to the following questions:
a. What would you like to have accomplished academically?
b. In which organizations and activities would you like to have been involved?
c. What do you want to experience personally and socially while in college?
d. What do you need to do to prepare yourself for your career beyond college?

2. Reflecting on that image of yourself portrayed in the above lists, what goals can you set for yourself to accomplish in the - next few months - next year - that will get you started toward what you hope to have accomplished as a graduating senior?

Reflections:

a. Was it difficult or easy to picture yourself as a graduating senior? Why? Why not?
b. Was it difficult or easy to identify what you would like to have accomplished academically and socially as a graduating senior? Why? Why not?
c. What struck you the most about yourself as a graduating senior?
d. Are you likely to follow-through on the goals you listed above? Why? Why not?
e. What impact could high risk alcohol consumption have on your ability to attain your goals?

Adapted from Activities Manual for The Education of Character, Lessons for Beginners, Will Keim (1995). Harcourt Brace College Publishers

Chapter Five

Acquaintance Rape

...removing the shroud of secrecy.

Why me?

Anonymous

I thought he just wanted to talk and before I knew it he was on top of me. There was nothing I could do. All I remember is that he reeked of booze.

Anonymous

Acquaintance Rape

I T IS ESTIMATED BY the United States Department of Justice that 154,000 rapes occur each year in the United States. One of the most common violent crimes on the campus today is acquaintance rape. In a 1998 study, about one in six college women reported being raped or the victim of an attempted rape.[32] In earlier studies between 15 and 30% of college women reported being the victims of rape.[33] Other research indicates higher percentages while still other research indicates lower percentages. One of the primary complications faced in conducting this type of research is that often victims of rape either do not report it for a variety of reasons or drop out of school. As a result we can suspect that the actual number of assaults may be more severe than some research indicates. Regardless of the exact number, everyone can agree that this is a serious problem which must be confronted.

Nature of the Problem

Initially referred to as date rape, today acquaintance rape is considered a more accurate term. The reason for this is simple. Research indicates that campus rapes occur not only between people who are on a date but also between those who simply know each other and are not dating. More than eight in ten victims know their attacker. They may have met at a party, or visited an off campus house with friends, or were simply socializing in each other's rooms in the residence hall, thus the term acquaintance rape. Remember, rape is rape and using the term acquaintance in no way suggests its effects are any less severe than with strangers.

As you read through the statistics in this section, understand they are referring to male on female attacks. In doing so, I do not wish to perpetuate the image of women in society as "victims" nor men as "predators," however, when it comes to sexual assault, more often than not women are the victims of the assault. For that reason, this section will deal with just that, male on female sexual assault. Rape, defined as forcing another person to engage in sexual intercourse (vaginal, anal or oral), can occur between different or same sex individuals. The bottom line for any of these tragedies is that more often than not, alcohol is involved.

> *I can't believe he did it. We were teammates. He just didn't seem like the kind of guy to do that kind of thing. I guess he just got too drunk. I really feel sorry for that girl.*
>
> David A., University of Miami senior

Impact of Alcohol

As previously indicated, alcohol is a depressant drug which impacts us in a number of debilitating ways. Simply put, a depressant drug slows down our central nervous system. As a result, alcohol can impair our ability to communicate. Therefore, men and women can often misinterpret what the other is trying to say or do. "Maybe later" becomes "yes." "No" becomes "give me a few more drinks first." An innocent kiss may be mistakenly viewed as an invitation to more intimate sexual contact. While under the influence of alcohol, verbal and non-verbal cues are frequently misinterpreted by college men and women, more often with men overestimating women's interest in them as sexual partners based on the woman's characteristics such as friendliness, attractiveness and clothing.[34]

Alcohol, as a depressant drug, may inhibit brain functions that control impulsive behavior. As a result, aggressive actions a perpetrator may not have engaged in while sober may now be acted upon, resulting in a violent attack. Additionally, alcohol is one of the only drugs that seems to actually contribute to aggressive, violent behavior in some individuals. In a study of female students who had been the victims of some type of sexual aggression (including rape, intimidation, illegal restraint) sixty eight per cent reported their male assailant had been drinking[35] or using other drugs before the crime and one in four admitted to being moderately or extremely intoxicated.[36] In another study, more than half the male students who admitted to having committed sexual assault said they had been drinking. Some may even use alcohol and other drugs to justify an assault.[37]

The blame for unwanted sexual behavior and sexual assault always lies with the perpetrator who made the choice to violate another person. But, alcohol, as a depressant drug, can also impair our judgment. As a result victims may place themselves in a high-risk environment which they may have avoided had they been sober. In saying this, I am not blaming the victim but rather pointing out the connection between alcohol use and risk. In a 1987 study more than half the women who reported being sexually assaulted also reported drinking or using drugs at the time of the assault. Additionally, in the same survey, approximately 20% of victims reported being moderately or severely intoxicated at the time of the assault.[38] In a later survey nearly three quarters of the college women indicating they had been sexually assaulted also reported consuming alcohol at the time of the assault. Again, this information is not meant to cast blame on the victim. What it does indicate is that victims of sexual assault are often rendered incapable of assessing a dangerous situation due, somewhat, to alcohol induced impairment.

I was so embarrassed I didn't want to talk to anyone. I just wanted to crawl into a hole and die.

Anonymous

If Assaulted

If you are raped or know someone who has been raped, there are some critical steps that should be followed. First of all, get help! As a result of the trauma of the attack, victims can rarely think clearly about what they can and should do. Either stay in your room and call for help or get to a safe place. If you are not yet comfortable going to officials, get help from a friend with whom you can talk. There are a number of support services available for rape victims on college campuses. Also, the local police usually have specially trained officers sensitive to the needs of a rape victim. Additionally, if for any reason you are not comfortable with campus services or the police, you can contact a local women's services organization in your community. Or, for a victims services office near you, call the Rape, Abuse and Incest National Network (RAINN), a national rape crisis hotline 1-800-656-4673.

Although dealing with the proper adjudication of the crime is not of immediate concern to a victim of rape, trying to maintain the integrity of evidence of the attack is crucial for future decisions about judicial procedures. If you choose to report the assault, first call the police, then go to the hospital. Do not shower, bathe or douche. Do not change your clothes however bring a change of clothes with you to either the police station or the hospital. The police will need the clothes you were wearing during the assault as evidence. When possible, do not straighten up your room or the area where the attack occurred until the medical and legal evidence has been collected. Failure to obtain evidence within 72 hours after an assault can limit the legal actions for the victim following the assault. While at the hospital, have medical personnel treat external and internal injuries as well as test for sexually transmitted diseases. Most hospitals have specially trained nurses who will administer a rape kit. Finally, if you suspect there is even the slightest chance that you were slipped some type of sedating drug, have a urine test taken. Even if you are not yet at a hospital or treatment facility, collect the first urine sample available in a clean container. There is now a federal law that can put a rapist in jail for 20 years if a sedating drug is used to commit the crime.

Yes, I know these instructions seem quite cold and calculating, but they are critical. The emotional turmoil and distress the victim experiences is certainly extremely painful, but following these steps will ensure that if the victim chooses to report and/or prosecute, there will be useful evidence. These steps are necessary to assist in ensuring that the attacker will be arrested and effectively prosecuted in court.

> *People tell me to get over it but they just don't understand.*
>
> Anonymous

> *I was having real problems afterwards. I eventually dropped out of school for awhile. My counselor and my family have been great. I don't think I could have gotten through this without them.*
>
> Jennie, Boston University

Long Term Consequences

As indicated earlier, professional help is of utmost importance not only for the immediate concerns regarding the attack but also the long term implications. Certainly the survivor of a rape is traumatized by the assault. More often than not, survivors develop Post Traumatic Stress Disorder (PTSD). Symptoms might include fear, helplessness, depression, anger and other emotional disturbances.

Additionally, we must not forget the long term impact can also be disturbing, often resulting in profound psychological and emotional difficulties. I have spoken with many—too many—students who are recovering from some type of sexual assault. Most are dealing with a number of similar issues:
-while most survivors have fears regarding their assailant, those assaulted while under the influence of a sedative drug (rohypnol, GHB, alcohol) will tend to develop a more generalized fear of men
- fear of intimacy
- extreme discomfort with any form of sexual activity
- fear of being in a confined area such as an elevator
- severe drop in Grade Point Average or perhaps even dropping out of college
- feelings of self-worth may be diminished
- feelings of loss of control over life experiences

A college campus presents a unique challenge in this situation. Since the attacker may also be a student in the school, the victim may experience ongoing anguish regarding the attack after seeing the attacker in class or around the campus.

Acquaintance Rape

Often the survivors of a rape will blame themselves for the attack. This could lead to other psychological difficulties. Also, there is the risk of pregnancy and sexually transmitted diseases. Finally, if there is a long, drawn out legal battle, this may once again victimize the survivor.

If you are the survivor of a rape or know someone who is, be sure to take advantage of the resources available to assist you or your friend. As indicated, rape has not only short term but also long term effects on the survivor:
- as you recover from the attack, attempt to define yourself as a survivor rather than a victim. This can be more empowering.
- individual counseling can help tremendously in dealing with the myriad of issues that can unfold over time.
- isolation could be one of your greatest enemies, so join a support group.
- you are not responsible for someone else's behavior nor can you change someone else but you can help yourself.

Ever since I was attacked, I have felt the need to help others by speaking out against all forms of violence.

Anonymous, University of Miami junior

Risk Reduction

Clearly, high risk alcohol use can have a major impact on the behavior of the drinker. Therefore, first and foremost, careful monitoring of your own alcohol consumption—if you choose to drink—is critical in avoiding acquaintance rape. Although misinterpretation is an important factor, most acquaintance rapes are planned ahead of time by the perpetrators.[39] By pressuring a date to drink heavily, the attacker can render his date less capable of resisting an assault.[40]

Besides minimizing your own alcohol consumption, there are a number of other steps you can take to confront this danger as well:
- many campuses offer escort services - use them! If your campus does not offer this type of service, work with your Student Activities Office, Counseling Services, Campus Security or any other organization that can implement an escort service.
- be sure you enter and leave a party with a friend. Commit to each other that, regardless of the circumstances, you will only leave a party with each other, and both of you will always maintain that commitment.
- women should avoid going to a room alone with a man especially if he has been drinking, even if it is her own room. If you do leave a social situation, tell a friend where you are going and when you expect to return. Cell phones can be used to maintain contact with friends as well.
- be assertive, direct and confident. Don't be afraid to be confrontational and do

not give mixed messages.
- being embarrassed is better than being raped. Scream if necessary.

Some drugs can be placed in drinks without the drinker knowing it. Here are some tips that can help you avoid being slipped some type of drug:
- Do not leave any drinks, alcoholic or not, unattended.
- Do not take any beverages, including alcohol, from someone you do not know well or trust.
- At a bar/club, only accept drinks from a bartender or waiter or waitress.
- Do not accept open container drinks from anyone.
- If you feel disproportionately impaired—meaning more impaired than you would normally be from the amount you have consumed—go to the emergency room immediately. Bring along a sample of your drink for analysis if possible.

Both men and women need to lookout for others who may be at risk due to their own impairment, or the impairment of their friends, and address the developing dangerous situation. Together they can also participate in campus and community advocacy groups that confront sexual assault and high risk drinking. Additionally, they can implement and/or support education programs about sexuality and acquaintance rape. Students, faculty and staff all need to maintain a high level of vigilance in scrutinizing how their administrators deal with sexual assault on their campus, especially the treatment of both the alleged perpetrators and the victims.

In closing, I must make a plea to the men reading this book. One of the most disturbing studies I have read regarding this topic was published in 1991. In this study college males were asked about their attitudes towards rape. The men were asked if they would commit acquaintance rape if they could be assured that no one else would find out and they would not be punished, Only 40% said they were not likely to rape a woman if given the opportunity described.[41] This is, to say the least, shocking. Although female students can take steps to minimize their risk for sexual assault, research suggests that sexual assault is much more associated with perpetrator characteristics than it is with victim characteristics. These characteristics include but are not limited to sexist attitudes towards women, a belief that their behavior is justifiable and a belief that men are entitled to sex under certain conditions such as a "reimbursement for paying for a date." [42]

Since in one study we see that one in fifteen men reported attempting rape or having committed rape, men must be considered as part of the solution to these repeated tragedies.[43] Men can be instrumental in addressing acquaintance rape and be a positive force for change on their campus by:
- assisting campus organizations in their development of education and prevention programs;

- speaking out regarding their own concerns about sexual assault, especially when it is raised in a humorous fashion;
- challenging sexist and violent attitudes;
- developing and implementing healthy and low risk party guidelines for campus organizations;
- carefully monitoring their own and their friends' alcohol consumption;
- avoiding, and helping other men avoid, risky situations which might place them in a position to be falsely accused of sexual assault.

Although this chapter has dealt primarily with male on female rape, men also get raped. It is estimated that men represent about 7% to 10% of all rape victims. Males are assaulted most often by other males. However, offenders who assault males are not primarily homosexual. About half of these offenders report having either heterosexual or bisexual preferences.

Male victims face similar physical dangers and emotional difficulties following a rape along with some additional challenges. Because our society still believes that males should be strong and able to protect themselves, males are less likely to report sexual victimization than females. Fear of embarrassment, ridicule and rejection along with feelings of inadequacy keep male victims from telling loved ones and reporting the crime. In assisting male survivors of rape, just like women, men need support and understanding if they are to recover from the assault.[44]   ◆

Addiction

... physical, chronic, and progressive disease.

"When I first got to college in the Fall I got drunk because it made me feel comfortable at parties. My drinking did not interfere with my academics. However when I returned in the Spring, I got drunk to get over the depression of a recent breakup. My grades suffered drastically and I realized I needed to slow down a bit. However, by my Junior year I was drinking nightly. I hit bottom around the end of last Spring semester. I felt like I was on a mission to self-destruct."   Anonymous

"I know I have to be careful 'cause I don't want to turn out like my father or grandmother. They both got sick from alcoholism and my grandmother died from it. I need to learn that I am not special or different from them. I can have problems in the future."   Anonymous

"I am a recovering alcoholic. I realized I was addicted to alcohol when I was seventeen. I wish the rest of the students in my dorm would understand that this stuff is real and it could happen to them."   Anonymous

Addiction

ONE OF THE QUESTIONS ASKED MOST FREQUENTLY by college students regarding drinking is, "What's the difference between a social drinker, a problem drinker and an alcoholic?" The complex nature of alcoholism or other drug addiction prohibits an extensive, in-depth look at this problem within the confines of this book. As a matter of fact, hundreds, if not thousands of books have been written about the topic. I'd like to suggest to you however, one excellent resource, Buzzed.[45] This book will provide you with a more comprehensive look at not only alcoholism and other drug addiction but also drug pharmocolgy. In the meantime, maybe I can give you some helpful guidelines to assist you in gaining a fundamental awareness of alcoholism.

When someone experiences problems as a result of their drinking, they are, at the very least, a problem drinker and are considered to be abusing alcohol. Is the problem drinker an alcoholic? It depends. An acceptable definition of alcoholism for most professionals is the continued consumption of alcohol despite the physical, psychological, and/or social problems caused by the drinking combined with an inability to consistently control the drinking occasions or the amount of alcohol consumed.

For example, a husband calls his wife to tell her he's stopping for a few beers at the bar on the way home from work. He arrives home drunk at three in the morning. This lack of control continues; it threatens his marriage and he loses his job. A college student may plan on going to parties and not getting drunk, but more often than not, the student gets drunk and passes out. Schoolwork suffers, classes are missed, and the student fails. In addition to the problems described in the Risks chapter of this book, a college student who is abusing alcohol may experience relationship problems with parents and friends, money problems, health problems, difficulty keeping a part-time job and/or many other more subtle problems due to drinking.

Both the husband and the student continue to drink despite the fact that drinking is causing these problems. According to the textbook definition, we could consider both of them alcoholics. The difficulty arises in actually diagnosing them as alcoholic or not. This diagnosis should be left to the professionals. As you can see, there is no real clear criteria for early differentiation between the problem drinker and the alcoholic. Someone who abuses alcohol experiences many of the same problems as the alcoholic and is not an alcoholic, yet. What we do know is that abuse of alcohol can lead to alcoholism. If you minimize your abuse of alcohol then you will minimize your risk for alcoholism.

Rather than confuse yourself with definitions and labels, it might serve you better to analyze what impact alcohol is having on your life. At the end of this chapter is a questionnaire that may help. It will not assess whether or not you are an alcoholic, but it will help you, at the very least, determine if alcohol is or is not affecting your life. If it is, then I suggest you make adjustments in your drinking patterns.

Following is a description of the behaviors associated with the phases of drinking. As you read through it, try to determine what phase you are in if you drink. You do not need to experience all of the issues to be considered in a particular phase. You might experience all or some of those things described in each phase.

PHASES OF DRINKING [46]

PHASE ONE: (Social Drinker)
- Joe and Jane may choose to drink once in awhile.
- When they do drink, they do not get impaired. Since they do not drink to impairment, there's no increase in their tolerance.
- There are no negative outcomes from their drinking.
- They have a take-it-or-leave-it attitude about drinking.

PHASE TWO: (Social Drinker)
- Jane and Joe enjoy drinking. They drink regularly, perhaps two or three times per week.
- When they do drink, they usually get impaired. Because they are drinking to impairment, their tolerance is increasing.
- There are no apparent negative outcomes from their drinking, except maybe a hangover once in awhile.
- They generally look forward to the weekend so they can "really let loose."

PHASE THREE: (Problem Drinker)
Early Phase:
- Jane and Joe drink regularly.
- They get impaired regularly. Their tolerance is continuing to increase.
- They arrive late for classes and sometimes cut classes due to drinking and/or hangovers.
- The quality of their school work is inconsistent. They are missing deadlines.
- They seem to be preoccupied with drinking.
- They might experience a blackout.

Middle Phase:
- Jane and Joe begin to cut classes regularly.
- They become unreliable. Their personal relationships begin to suffer from disagreements with roommates, teammates and/or friends.
- They avoid situations where there is no drinking.
- They become ill more frequently.
- They experience more money problems.
- They drink in the morning once in awhile to cure their hangovers.

Late Phase:
- Jane and Joe cut classes a week at a time.
- At times their attitudes are belligerent and aggressive or passive and withdrawn.
- They experience many personal problems with friends and family.
- They have more money problems. Maybe they get a job to support their partying.
- They may get a DUI violation or encounter serious trouble with school administration.
- Their academic performance may deteriorate drastically.

PHASE FOUR: (Addicted to Alcohol: Alcoholic)
- Jane and Joe become totally undependable. They experience serious family and other relationship problems.
- They drink to cure their withdrawal from alcohol.
- They experience serious legal difficulties.
- They get suspended or drop out of school.
- They experience many other negative outcomes.

Can you consume alcohol and not experience any serious alcohol problems? As you can see, drinkers in Phase Two may be doing just that. They are out drinking, getting impaired yet not experiencing any problems. But—and it's a huge but—as explained earlier, each time you drink to impairment your tolerance increases. We know that if you continue to drink to impairment, your tolerance will continue to increase. As a result, you will eventually move to Phase Three and possibly Phase Four. That is why increasing tolerance is always an indicator of increased risk for alcoholism.[47] The student who brags about his or her ability to consume excessive quantities of alcohol is actually revealing, and ignorantly bragging about, his or her increased risk for alcoholism.

Many students believe that high risk drinking in college is simply an expected phase of life they go through—that it is a rite of passage. Many believe they will simply discontinue their high risk consumption after they graduate. Does "I'll quit when I graduate" sound familiar? Research indicates that this is not always the case. Based on a 27-year follow-up of college students begun in 1950, we see that 50 percent of those students who drank five or more drinks on four or more days per week while in college experienced alcoholism or other serious alcohol-related problems twenty years later.[48] Today, unfortunately, many more students fit this drinking profile than was true when this study began.

Long before drug addiction including alcoholism is a physical disease with physical cravings, it's an emotional and psychological disease. At first you may choose when and where and what to drink, but once you have started using there could come a point at which you can no longer choose whether to continue. At that point, the choice belongs to the disease, and the disease will always choose its own survival over yours. If you find yourself in this situation, help is there for the asking, but you must ask. Reach for the telephone, reach for the telephone book, look under Alcoholism or Drug Abuse, (or Alcoholics Anonymous) pick a number, and dial it. Someone at the other end is waiting to hear from you. ◆

Addressing a temperance meeting, Abraham Lincoln said,"If we take the habitual drunkards as a class, their heads and hearts will bear an advantageous comparison with those of any other... the demon of intemperance seems ever to have delighted in sucking the blood of genius and generosity."

Chapter 6 Addictions:

Identifying Alcohol Problems

Goal:

To assess the role alcohol may be playing in your life.

Instructions:

Circle word that best describes your answer to the following questions. Within the past three months:

Yes No Did you miss class because of drinking or hangovers?

Yes No Did you drink to overcome shyness and to build confidence?

Yes No Did you drink to escape from study or home worries?

Yes No Did it bother you if someone said you drank too much?

Yes No Did you need to have a drink before you went out on a date?

Yes No Did you ever have money problems due to alcohol consumption?

Yes No Did your friends drink less than you?

Yes No Did you ever have a memory loss due to drinking?

Yes No Did you get into trouble with residential life staff due to drinking?

Yes No Did you always drink until the bottle was empty, all the beer cans were dead or until the party is over?

Yes No Did you ever think you had a drinking problem?

Yes No Did drinking affect your reputation?

Scoring for this exercise can be found in the Challenge Results Section at the end of this book.

Reflections:

After completing the survey, ask yourself the following questions:

a. How do you feel about the results of this survey?

b. What role does alcohol play in your life?

c. Is alcohol having a negative impact on your college career?

d. Do you know what campus resources are available to assist people with alcohol or other drug problems?

Chapter Seven

Intervention

... if not you, who?

... if not now, when?

"Once I talked to my boyfriend about his excessive drinking. It turned into a battle ground."

Amy S., Plymouth State College sophomore

"I don't know how to approach the person. I'm afraid of not getting through and perhaps even making an enemy."

Terrence J., Manhattan College senior

Intervention

I F IT HASN'T HAPPENED ALREADY, sooner or later someone close to you will experience a problem with alcohol or other drugs. While in college it may be a roommate, a teammate, a loved one or a friend. Beyond college it might be a relative, perhaps your father or mother, an employer, an employee, a future spouse or maybe a son or daughter. I guarantee that it will happen.

When confronted with this situation, we tend to feel helpless and hopeless. After all, conventional wisdom states that you need to wait for the person to hit bottom before he or she will seek help. But conventional wisdom isn't always wise, especially when it comes to alcohol and other drugs. You may not be able to help someone who has an alcohol problem until that person hits bottom, but you can *raise the bottom.*

When

> *"How do I know if she is an alcoholic? She now vomits blood, complains of stomach problems and drinks almost every night until she stumbles home. Sometimes she even drives home. How can I be sure she is an alcoholic?"*
>
> Anonymous

As indicated in the "Addiction" chapter of this book, it is difficult to assess whether or not someone is actually addicted to alcohol. But, that should not be the question you are asking yourself. If drinking is causing problems in someone's life then the person should be confronted about the drinking. In the situation cited above, it is obvious that the drinking is causing problems. Is the person an addict? We do not know—but she definitely needs immediate help.

You don't need to wait—you shouldn't wait—until a more serious problem arises. You don't need to wait until the person hits bottom. That's like saying if you had a friend or loved one perched on the edge of a bridge ready to jump—ready to commit suicide—you would allow the person to jump, then run down to where your friend hit the bottom and pick up the pieces. Consider this: If not now, when? If not you, who?

Look back at the Phases of Drinking. During what phase would you confront someone about their drinking? Most well-intentioned friends or relatives might confront Joe or Jane in Phase Two. And that might seem to be an appropriate time. However, as much as we would like to see it, we should not expect them to change their behavior if they are in Phase Two. After all, they are drinking, having a good time and are experiencing no apparent negative outcomes. In their minds, they believe that drinking is harmless and fun—that they have everything under control. This does not mean we should not say something to them. Their tolerance is rising, and they will probably experience problems sooner or later. They need to be informed that their increased tolerance is an indication of increased risk.

If you confront them in Early Phase Three, there are more concrete reasons for them to examine their drinking. They are experiencing negative outcomes, and these can be highlighted as reasons for considering a reduction in consumption. Also, their tolerance is becoming dangerously high. They are continuing to come closer to their trigger level for alcoholism.

How

"This information was very helpful when I confronted my friend. This could help save the lives of many college students."
John S., Keene State College senior

"My friend made it clear to his girlfriend that he was doing this because he cared about her."
Ralph S., Franklin Pierce College sophomore

"How can I approach him without getting him upset?"
Anonymous

Intervention

"I don't like seeing my friend hurting herself over and over, but she really doesn't think she has a problem. When anyone does say anything she gets defensive."

Anonymous

Alcoholism is considered to be the disease of denial. But the seeds of denial are planted long before the actual addiction. There are ways to break through the denial. Here are some guidelines to follow when confronting someone you believe has an alcohol or other drug problem.

- *Be well-informed about alcohol.* There are professionals on most campuses trained to work with students and their alcohol concerns. Some campuses offer academic courses about alcohol and other drugs.

- *Choose your time and place carefully.* Confront the person in private and when the person is sober.

- *Expect denial.* Most people experiencing problems with alcohol have developed an intricate web of psychological defenses. These defenses manifest themselves in the form of denial of the problem.

- *Be confident and positive.* Indicate you care for the person but not the behavior.

- *Call for help when necessary.* Friends, residential life staff, relatives and/or counselors can be of valuable assistance. In some situations an organized intervention coordinated by a professional health care worker may be necessary.

- *Get help for yourself.* Relatives and friends of people experiencing alcohol problems also experience their own difficulties. Find help through your own friends or support groups such as Al-Anon.

- *Choose your words carefully.* Don't label the person. Avoid terms like alcoholic or problem drinker. Simply state that the drinking is causing problems.

Here's a framework within which you can present your concerns. This may make your confrontation more acceptable to the drinker.

Intervention

"I care ..." Indicate your care and concern for the person. For instance: "I love you." "You are my best friend." "I care about you."

"I see ..." Describe the specific behaviors that concern you. For instance: "For the past three weekends you have gotten into a fight after drinking." "You have missed class every Friday morning for the past five weeks because you were hungover."

"I feel ..." Describe how you feel. For instance: "I'm concerned that you are going to fail out of school." "I'm worried about our relationship." "I get angry when I know I can't count on you."

Listen ... Give the person an opportunity to respond.

"I'd like ..." Indicate what you'd like the person to do. For instance: "I'd like you to go to the Counseling Center." "I'd like you to stop coming over here when you are drunk."

"I will ..." Offer your support and indicate what you will do to assist the person. For instance: "I'll find out about what professional assistance is available." "I'll go with you to see the counselor."

You can be sure that if you confront someone regarding their alcohol or other drug use, their immediate response will not be "Thanks for pointing that out. I'll go see a counselor right away." More often than not the response will be some form of denial:

Excuses: "I've been really stressed out lately." "I'm carrying 18 credits and need to loosen up when I can." "We lost the game by two points."

Anger: "Get off my case." "Up yours!"

Blame: "My boyfriend has been really bugging me lately." "I had a tough test today." "My professors are too demanding."

Projection: "Yeah right, well what about you?" "So what, this is college. Everyone drinks."

Minimizing: "It's no big deal." "I've got it under control."

Intervention

If you are serious about helping someone, you need to understand that success in this situation comes in a variety of forms. Obviously, if the drinker were to agree with you, seek help and reduce the drinking, you were extremely successful. Great! There are also other levels of success. The person may simply agree and decrease the consumption but not seek professional help. And that might be OK.

However, the person may simply agree but make no changes. Is this failure? No! Most people in rehabilitation say they sought help because a friend and/or relatives suggested they seek help. For many of them, it may have taken up to thirty confrontations before the person actually sought help. In your situation, maybe you are the first person to confront the problem drinker, and maybe you are the tenth, but maybe you are the thirtieth—the person might finally make the move. At the very least, despite the denial, the person will never drink again without having your concern echo in the back of his or her mind. And that helps!

Enabling

"My boyfriend had serious problems with alcohol. But I always tried to make him happy. I always tried to fix his problems. Thank goodness I stopped doing this because it only made me feel worse and certainly didn't really help him."

Anonymous

"I guess in a sense I was an enabler. I was always taking responsibility for his actions which I guess made things worse."

Carla J., University of Maryland first-year student

A behavior pattern that's easy to fall into if you have a friend or relative with an alcohol problem is *enabling*. Enabling is the process of removing the normal consequences of drinking from the drinker. The wife who calls her husband's boss and claims he has the flu when he is really hungover is enabling his drinking. The enabler shelters the drinker from the drinking problems. The drinker fails to see the drinking as a problem when the enabler provides protection from the consequences of drinking. The drinker then fails to see the need for help. Enabling can be defined quite simply as "good intentions with harmful results."

Students tend to believe they are helping their friends when they enable in the following ways:

- Make excuses for the drinking behavior
- Obtain notes from classes missed by the drinker due to her drinking or hangover
- Lend money for alcohol purchases
- Submit projects for the drinker because she was too hungover to make it to class
- Buy alcohol for the drinker
- Try to occupy the drinker's time so there won't be time to drink
- Blame the drinking on friends or circumstances
- Drink with the person so you can watch over him when he is drinking
- Vow not to do any of the above yet find yourself doing it again

These may seem like friendly gestures, but they simply contribute to further drinking. Why should the drinker make any changes if there are no perceived problems due to the drinking?

Detachment

> *"I feel awful for just giving up on him, but I tried for three and one-half years to help him and failed in my efforts to do so. I tried to be a good friend and it seems all I got were huge amounts of frustration."*
>
> Anonymous

> *"It was very difficult to walk away from someone I cared about, but it came to the point where it was the only solution."*
>
> Anonymous

Intervention

There may come a time when you believe you can no longer associate with the drinker while he or she is using. Only you know when this time has been reached. It is extremely important that you let the person know why you are severing the ties of your friendship. Do not simply avoid the drinker. If you do, he or she will probably project the problem back onto you. Let the drinker know how you feel. Use the process suggested above. Then, at some point you may need to *lovingly* detach from the drinker if the situation becomes too difficult for you. Yes, this can be extremely difficult. But what is your choice? Finally, be sure to leave the door open for the time when the person may finally agree to seek help.   ♦

Personal Challenge: Intervening

1. Do you know someone you believe has an alcohol or other drug problem?
2. Do you believe you should confront this person?
3. What reaction can you anticipate? How might you be able to deal with this reaction?
3. Are there any resources available to help educate you about the nature of your relationship with this person and his/her alcohol or other drug problem?
4. Is there anyone who can assist you in confronting this person about their alcohol or other drug problem?
5. What resources can you recommend to this person for assistance with his/her problem?

Chapter Eight

Family Issues

... why does it still hurt?

"I've started to understand why my father feels the way he does. My dad is a great person but he still shows the scars from when he was abused when he was growing up. Alcoholism is a big problem in this country and it effects many people other than the alcoholic—the children, the spouses and the friends are all sucked into the problem."

Anonymous

"When my dad was drinking heavily he once threatened to blow my mother's head off. Somehow he had gotten his gun and locked himself in the bathroom. Me and my sister were downstairs and heard everything."

Anonymous

"I hated her for being the way she was. I did not think it was fair to have a mother who could not remember her own daughter's name."

Anonymous

"The problem is that when she's not drinking she's the best mother. When I see her drinking I block it out and think of what she's like when she's not drunk."

Anonymous

Family Issues

ALCOHOLISM AFFECTS MORE PEOPLE than just the alcoholic. It has the potential to destroy the basic fabric of family life. And, recent research indicates that many of your peers come from families that have experienced some difficulties with alcohol or other drug use. Results of the 1997-1998 Core Alcohol and Drug Survey indicate:

- 5 percent of college students have a mother with some alcohol or other drug-related problem
- 15 percent of college students have a father with some alcohol or other drug-related problem
- 12.1 percent of college students have a maternal grandparent with some alcohol or other drug-related problem
- 11.4 percent of college students have a paternal grandparent with some alcohol or other drug-related problem
- 25 percent of college students have an aunt or uncle with some alcohol or other drug-related problem
- 9.8 percent of college students have a brother or sister with some alcohol or other drug-related problem[49]

These were the students who were able to identify the problems as related to alcohol or other drugs. Based on my interaction with students, I'm sure many more are experiencing similar situations but have not identified them as related to alcohol or other drug use.

Unspoken Rules

"Shame, embarrassment, humiliation, guilt, anger, hurt, disappointment ... and on and on. I experienced it all."

Kevin W., Keene State College senior

"There were so many secrets and difficulties with feelings. I never got to know my real SELF. (You know what I mean?) All of these problems were in our family and here I am now trying to cope with them."

Anonymous

"I was never told what to feel. I was told to stop feeling. Instead of talking about our disagreements we would 'forget' about them."

Anonymous

"My mother hit me but I went out on the date anyway. I had a black eye and bruises and as an excuse I told my friends I was in a football game with my brother."

Anonymous

"I lied to my father about my mother's drinking. I don't know if I ever forgave myself for covering up for her. I wonder that maybe if I told my father the truth he would have made her get help."

Christopher T., University of New Hampshire junior

The family of an alcoholic experiences many difficulties. In order to deal with these difficulties, many alcoholic families develop very similar behavior patterns or unspoken rules, "Don't talk, don't feel, don't trust." These patterns are coping mechanisms for an impossible situation:

- **Don't talk** to anyone about our problem. Don't embarrass the family. We are the only ones with this problem. Don't tell your teacher, a counselor or even your friends. Later in life, adult children of alcoholics tend to have difficulty communicating within relationships.

- **Don't feel,** because your feelings will just get squashed. Why get excited over my birthday, Mom will just get drunk and ruin the party. If I cry they tell me to stop crying and grow up.

- **Don't trust** Dad. He always says he'll show up at the game but usually ends up in the bar. Serious mistrust of others can follow the child of an alcoholic into adulthood.

Family Issues

Results

"Intimate relationships have always been difficult for me. Even though my current boyfriend and I are somewhat successful, there are problems with our intimacy and communication. Just about every person I have been involved with has some serious dysfunction in their family."

Jennifer N., St. Michael's College senior

"I know I am always looking for approval but when I get it I can't accept it."

Anonymous

"I never have any real fun like my friends."

Anonymous

"I wonder if my father would be a more feeling person if he quit drinking. My house is very cold and I don't mean the weather kind of cold. Because of this coldness we are all that way even outside of our home. It is really kind of sad."

Anonymous

The pain associated with growing up in an alcoholic family can have serious deleterious effects on an individual even into adulthood. Many of your peers are arriving at college with more "baggage" than is apparent. They may have difficulty confiding in you even though you consider yourself a close friend. Maybe they will jump from one bed to another searching for a meaningful relationship through a variety of meaningless sexual encounters. Maybe they will drown their fears and pain in alcohol and other drugs. Maybe they will take the time and make the effort to grow while in college despite their past difficulties.

Growth

"Lately I have been wondering how being the child of an alcoholic has affected me. I've been unhappy with myself for certain personality characteristics of mine that make my life complicated. I hope that some day I have the time and courage to evaluate the situation and do something about it."

Anonymous

"My mom comes from an alcoholic family. It was tough for her but she turned out great! She's successful and one of the best moms I know. It can be a lot of heartache but it's not hopeless."

Karla N., Keene State College first-year student

"I have accepted my father for what he was. He probably did the best he could. I do not need to accept his behavior nor create any more pain for myself. I am now free of his influence."

Anonymous

"Trusting others begins with trusting myself. That's easier said than done."

Anonymous

"It was difficult for a long time to know who was actually my father, the man who was loving and caring or the man who was so abusive and at times dangerous. Finally he got a lot of help and went through therapy and now, with medication and counseling he is the father I never knew. Sure it has caused me some problems but I'm working them out."

Anonymous

Yes, if you are the child of an alcoholic, your family life may have been difficult, perhaps excruciating. Yes, maybe those difficulties are still affecting you today. And yes, you can do something about it. It is important to realize that you can "turn the page" on that part of your life. You can now take control of your life and cease being a victim. As a matter of fact, now may be a great time to confront these issues. Of course, this is easier said than done. Get help. Join a support group. Speak to a counselor. Talk to a friend. It's never too late. Sure it takes courage, but what have you got to lose? Don't have the time? Do you have time to continue being miserable? I think not! You have a whole life ahead of you, and you deserve the best.

Take the time to work on yourself. Don't escape into the black hole of alcohol or other drugs. Don't hide behind a beer mask, a fake smile, or an arrogant attitude. Find out who you are and be true to yourself. Sure life is difficult, but with a little help from a counselor, a support group and/or your friends, it can also be wonderful.

Family Issues

Risks

"It's odd how each of us reacted differently to my father's drinking. My brother is an alcoholic. My sister never drinks. My oldest sister had a serious problem with bed wetting. Right now I drink a lot but believe I have it under control."

Anonymous

"The reason all this concerns me so much is that my father is an alcoholic as is a good portion of his side of the family. I wonder how that will affect me and my children."

Mary O., Notre Dame College senior

So, is alcoholism genetic? The jury is still out on that one. However, we do know that the child of an alcoholic is at greater risk for developing alcoholism—**four times greater!** This increased risk, sometimes described as a predisposition to alcoholism, is the result of a number of factors including:

Biological risk level: Just as we inherit a certain likelihood of heart disease, we are all born with some biological level of risk for alcoholism. And for some of us, that risk is increased. Those of us with a biological history of alcoholism in our family are at greater biological risk for alcoholism.[50]

Biological response: Research on brain-wave patterns of children of alcoholics (COAs) following alcohol consumption indicates a greater relaxation effect from the alcohol. The startle reflex of the COA is slower after alcohol consumption. This seems to reflect a more pleasurable response from alcohol.[51]

Initial tolerance: COAs tend to have high initial tolerance to alcohol. This combined with a lower trigger level for alcoholism indicates that the COA

Alexander the Great was an alcoholic. He may have
become addicted to wine under the influence of his father
King Philip II of Macedon, also a heavy drinker.

does not have as many opportunities to drink to impairment before increasing the tolerance so much that it goes beyond the trigger level for alcoholism.[52]

Metabolism: A by-product of the metabolism of alcohol is acetaldehyde.
Acetaldehyde is thought to be involved in some way with addiction. When
COAs metabolize alcohol there are increased levels of acetaldehyde.[53]

So here's the trap for children of alcoholics. They are born with a greater biological risk for alcoholism. They are usually born with a high tolerance, meaning
they are getting a head start on the development of alcoholism. When they drink,
it feels very pleasurable but they are also producing an increased level of a product, acetaldehyde, that is possibly linked to addiction. Children of alcoholics may
think they have it under complete control—but do they? None of us can control
our biological response to alcohol. ◆

Family Issues

Personal Challenge: Family Health

Goal:

To examine the role alcohol may or may not have had on your family.

Instructions:

For each of the following characteristics, circle TRUE or FALSE based on how well they describe your family.

1. All feelings are all right to express.	True	False
2. All subjects are open to discussion.	True	False
3. Individual differences are accepted.	True	False
4. What you do is more important than who you are	True	False
5. Everyone must conform to the dominant person's ideas.	True	False
6. The atmosphere is generally tense.	True	False
7. Each person is responsible for his/her actions.	True	False
8. There are clear and flexible rules.	True	False
9. People feel loved and loving.	True	False
10. There are lots of "shoulds."	True	False
11. People feel tired and stressed.	True	False
12. Growth and change are discouraged.	True	False

Scoring for this exercise can be found in the Challenge Results Section at the end of this book.

Reflections:

A healthy family environment provides for children's needs in a way that promotes normal emotional, physical, and social development. High risk alcohol use by family member(s) can have a negative impact on family health.
1. Is your family healthy/unhealthy, functional/dysfunctional? Why/ why not?
2. What dysfunctional characteristics are present in your family? How do these affect YOUR personality? How might they be modified?

3. Children of dysfunctional families often become chemically dependent. Why do you think this happens?

4. What resources for students dealing with family problems are available on your campus? If you were having problems with your family, would you use these resources? Why or why not?

Adapted from Making Choices: A Personal Look at Alcohol & Drug Use (1992). McGraw-Hill Higher Education, Quinn/Scaffa

Chapter Nine

Recovery

... one day at a time.

"I sat and looked around the room. A lot of these people were just like me."

Stacey R., Keene State College junior

"One woman talked about how she started drinking in college. I thought to myself, what about me?"

Sean O., Keene State College junior

Recovery

I N ADDITION TO ATTENDING PARTIES and abstaining from alcohol, students in our alcohol-education program are required to attend meetings conducted by Alcoholics Anonymous or other Twelve Step programs such as Narcotics Anonymous. Twelve Step groups are support groups for people who are recovering from alcohol and/or other drug addiction. Another type of Twelve Step program is Al-Anon, a support group for friends or relatives of addicts.

Many students report that attending these meetings was one of the most valuable experiences in their college career. Based on the wide range of types of people attending the meetings, they quickly realize that alcoholism and other drug addictions can happen to anyone. They also learn through Al-Anon that the addictions affect not only the addict but also the family and friends of the addict.

Interacting with the people at the meetings provides them with a learning experience they won't forget. It gives them a first-hand look at the devastation caused by addiction—a devastation that can happen to them if they are not careful about their alcohol and/or other drug use. It personalizes alcoholism. In addition, they learn that there is help and support for those who develop an addiction or who have loved ones who have. Here are some reactions to the meetings:

> "There were a few who looked like they had been dragged through the field a few times, but other than that, the others looked quite normal. I tried not to stereotype or pre-judge, I just didn't know what to expect. Television portrays them much worse looking than they really are."

> "When you enter the meeting people are accepting you already without even knowing you."

"The meetings opened my eyes to what is out there and that 'bad' really does exist."

"There were young and old people and those that appeared rich and poor as well."

"I realized my life has just as much potential for disaster as theirs."

"Members picked up chips which represented the number of days they had been sober. They each gave a speech about how sobriety has changed their lives."

"There was a woman there who was 23 years old. She said she had been sober for 7 years. This means she was an alcoholic at age 16. She started drinking at age 11. When I saw that I sat back and asked myself when did I start drinking?"

"There was a 15 year old boy there who said he started going to these meetings after his best friend died of alcohol poisoning."

"I think I learned a lot from these meetings. When things aren't going so well for me, I think to myself about those people. They have had some real problems and got through them, so can I."

"Everyone was so supportive and respectful of each other."

"You could just feel the warmth and acceptance in the air. People helping people. Being there to lend a hand."

"You can tell that the listeners really care about what the speaker is saying. They don't care who you are or where you're from, they'll support you no matter what."

"I attended a meeting in my hometown. I saw a guy I had graduated from high school with. I thought, 'No way, he's not like this!' I talked to him later. It was interesting to find out how he hid his problem. I mean, he was the type of kid who played a sport and had excellent grades, yet he had a problem."

Some students find the references to God and/or a Higher Power during the meeting disconcerting. They quickly label the program as religious. Although Twelve Step programs are spiritually oriented, they have no religious affiliation at all. You can even be an atheist and follow the program.

> "I felt uncomfortable because it did seem very religious and I am not a very religious person."

> "I found it to be a very spiritual experience."

> "I gained a lot from this meeting. It was spiritual, supportive and confidential."

12 Step Meeting Guidelines

If you are at all interested in this topic, I urge you to attend one of these meetings. For further information about contacting Alcoholics Anonymous see the "Resources" section at the end of this book. Here are a few suggestions if you decide to attend a meeting:

- Attend only meetings that are designated as Open Meetings. You can find out if it is an Open Meeting by calling the local AA Hotline found in the front your telephone book. When entering the meeting, double check and ask someone if it is an Open Meeting.

- Confirm the time and location. Arrive at least 10 minutes early.

- If you go with someone else, only two of you should go together.

- Expect to feel nervous before entering. It is natural to feel this way when entering most new environments.

- If asked by anyone at the meeting why you are there, simply respond that you are visiting. Remember, your reason for being at the Open Meeting is hopefully a sincere desire to learn more about alcoholism and the support that is available for recovery.

- Anonymity is the foundation of AA. Situations and events may be discussed with one another but never discuss people or use their names. Do not take a notebook, recorder or other type devices.

- Use only first names, including yours. This protects everyone's anonymity.

- At most meetings a collection basket is circulated to help pay for coffee, cups, etc. A contribution is not expected, but if you do choose to contribute 25-50 cents is adequate unless you would like to contribute more.

- At some meetings a raffle is also held to cover the costs of books, flyers, brochures, etc. One dollar will usually get you a raffle ticket(s). Just like the other collection, you are not expected to participate and can easily choose to abstain.

- Be respectful and courteous at all times. This is a matter of life and death for the participants.

Many of my students state they feel as if they are intruding on the lives of the members when attending the meetings. These feelings are normal and actually make sense. Quite honestly, the things you will hear may sometimes be disturbing. When hearing someone discuss the tragedies associated with their addiction, you may very well feel as if you are intruding on their life. But, understand that the act of speaking openly about these tragedies in front of a group of friends and strangers is not only helpful to the audience but also to the speaker as well. Part of the recovery and support process is to share experiences, strengths and hopes with others including non-alcoholics. This is the AA process. You are not only allowed but welcome to attend Open Meetings. ♦

Chapter Ten

Greeks, Women and Athletes

... special concerns.

"Being a member of a fraternity on campus I believe I have been exposed to more drugs and alcohol than a non-Greek."
Dave C., Massachusetts Institute of Technology junior

"My girlfriend tries to keep up with me but I guess she just can't handle her booze."
Jack B., Daniel Webster College sophomore

Greeks, Women and Athletes

MEMBERS OF CAMPUS SPECIAL-INTEREST ORGANIZATIONS tend to be very protective of their group's reputation. And, when it comes to alcohol problems on their campus, they like to blame the other groups for the difficulties. Residential Life blames the fraternities and sororities, the Greeks in turn blame the athletes, the athletes blame the alumni, and, of course, everyone blames the first-year students. All groups experience some degree of difficulty regarding alcohol, some more than others.

Greeks

> *"Greek life has helped me with my self-esteem. Our community service not only helps other people it helps us too."*
>
> Steve V., Keene State College senior

> *"The Greeks are getting a lot smarter. They seem much more concerned. They provide alternative drinks. They provide escort service for those who need it. Granted they shouldn't be over-serving but at least they are making some improvements."*
>
> Melissa I., Keene State College junior

Membership in a fraternity or sorority provides many opportunities for leadership development, academic improvement, socialization, fun, community service and personal growth. Fraternities and sororities can also be the source of a large degree

> The "speakeasy" got its name because one had to whisper the code word through a slot in a locked door to gain admittance. Knowing the right word or the right person carried prestige.

of high risk activity. Presenting the following information is not meant as an attack nor a condemnation of Greek Life. However, in revealing this information I hope to challenge and consequently motivate Greek organizations to confront the one issue that consistently sheds a negative light on Greek Life, high risk alcohol consumption. As identified by one leading college reseacher, "If, from an alcohol risk point of view, the college campus is a dangerous place, then the fraternity houses are the 'Bermuda Triangle' of the campus ocean."[54] "Fraternity or sorority members are significantly more likely than other college students to endorse 'less-than-responsible' attitudes about alcohol."[55]

A large national study of binge drinking found that sorority members were almost twice as likely to be binge drinkers compared with nonsorority women (62 percent compared with 35 percent). Among men, 75 percent of fraternity members were binge drinkers, whereas 45 percent of other male students were.[56] This heavy and frequent drinking has a damaging impact on the health, safety and academic environment not only for the binge drinkers but also for the entire fraternity or sorority. In a related study, nearly half (45 percent) of fraternity residents and a fifth (19 percent) of sorority residents reported suffering five or more alcohol-related problems since the start of the school year. Only 17 percent of male and 11 percent of female students not involved in the Greek system had experienced as many problems. This study also revealed that 83 percent of fraternity residents and 78 percent of sorority residents reported having their studying or sleep interupted in the previous year because of another person's drinking while less than half of men (42 percent) and women (38 percent) not involved in the Greek system reported the same negative experience with other people's drinking. Finally, three times as many fraternity residents as nonmember male students reported being pushed, hit or assaulted in the previous year by someone who was intoxicated (34 percent versus 13 percent). And, twice as many sorority residents as nonmember females reported being pushed, hit or assaulted.[57]

> McSorley's Old Ale House in New York City was one of the last "for men only" drinking establishments. For over a century it displayed signs reading "Good ale, raw onions and no ladies" and "No Back Room in Hire for Ladies." In the wake of the feminist movement, McSorley's was sued for sexism and had to open its doors to women on August 10, 1970.

Greeks, Women and Athletes

If you are interested in membership in a Greek organization be sure to investigate its true character. If drinking alcohol is a primary focus of the organization, then your time spent with your new found sisters or brothers will be wasted. Don't join one simply because it has a reputation for great parties. Speak to other students and administrators about the group. Talk to alumni/ae about what the organization means to them now.

Be sure the members of the organization will accept you for who you are—not who they want you to be or how well you can handle your booze. If you are required to consume alcohol as a part of the membership process, I suggest you look for another organization. The group does not have your best interest in mind. Ninety percent of fraternity and sorority hazing accidents that result in death are related to alcohol use.[58]

Thankfully, as we move into the twenty first century, national fraternities and sororities have taken a long hard look at the impact alcohol has had on the health, safety and success of their members. Alcohol has disappeared from the houses of many organizations. Many groups now require alcohol and other drug education and abuse prevention programs for their members. Effective party management guidelines have been implemented by many organizations. Fraternities and sororities have made tremendous strides in taking action to minimize the impact alcohol has on its members, other students, the campus and the communities in which they reside.

> During the time of the kings and in the earliest days of the Republic, Roman women were forbidden to drink wine on pain of death. Male chauvinist Roman men thought that wine was too good to waste on women.

Women

Compared to thirty years ago, women's roles in society have expanded dramatically. There are more opportunities for work, for leadership and for equal pay for equal work. I am not saying it *is* equal, but there has been a great deal of progress in reaching equality. However, one thing a woman will never be able to do is "drink like a man." Nor, for that matter, will a man ever be able to drink like a woman. Males and females react to alcohol a bit differently.

Here's why. First of all, women tend to be smaller than men. Also, women tend to have a different body fluid content and a larger proportion of fat content than men. As a result, drink for drink, women will have a higher concentration of alcohol in their bloodstream due to the different levels of fat and body fluids of men and women. More important, however, is the difference in the way men and women metabolize alcohol. When the alcohol reaches the stomach it goes through what's called "first pass" metabolism. A small quantity of the alcohol is metabolized in the stomach even before it reaches the bloodstream through the small intestine. This first pass metabolism occurs due to the presence of the enzyme alcohol dehydrogenase (ADH). Women have less ADH than men. There is some evidence that this decreased level of ADH may result in women absorbing almost one third more alcohol than men from each drink.

Many women drink wine coolers, which often contain more alcohol than beer. Women possibly absorb up to one third more alcohol than men do, and their body makeup often results in a higher concentration of the alcohol in their bloodstream. No wonder women seem to be unable to handle alcohol like men. (Of course this is not the case for women who have developed increased tolerance to alcohol due to continued high risk alcohol consumption.) There are long-term consequences for women as well. Women become addicted sooner, they develop alcohol-related problems earlier and they die younger compared to men with similar drinking patterns.[59]

But some women seem to be determined to be as ignorant as some men when it comes to alcohol consumption. The onset of alcohol consumption by women is occurring earlier. Women are also drinking more alcohol. More than one third of college women reported drinking for the sole purpose of getting drunk in 1993, more than triple the 10 percent in 1977.[60] This shift in attitude by women is extremely risky since we know that women develop liver disease in a shorter period of time and at lower levels of consumption than men. Additionally, research indicates that a woman's risk for a fatal car crash is twice that of a man's when her blood alcohol level is between .05 percent and .14 percent.

Here are two other factors women need to consider if they choose to drink. Premenstrual hormonal changes can cause intoxication to set in faster during the days just before a woman gets her period. Also, some birth control pills or medication with estrogen will increase the level of intoxication for a woman who is drinking. So, if you fall into one or both of these two categories, you need to be extra careful about your alcohol decisions.

Greeks, Women and Athletes

Athletes

*"We drink during the week but never the night before a game.
We want to be ready."*

Anonymous

"The connection between beer and athletics is longstanding. It dates back to a period when beer was perceived as and consumed for refreshment more than for intoxication. A 1909 ad for Budweiser, under the headline Ball Players Use Beer in Training, quoted C.H. Ebbets, president of the Brooklyn Trolley Dodgers (later the Brooklyn Dodgers and still later the Los Angeles Dodgers) describing the ideal meal for his team: 'We would request a simple dinner with light beer as that is our idea of a proper drink for athletes in training'."[61] And yet, "In Austria, laws prohibit all public references at sporting events to alcoholic beverages. In a country that brews some of the most beautiful beer in the world, the very idea of a brewery involved with sports is considered appalling. 'We would never think of it,' huffs Dr. Klaus Leistner, director of the Austrian ski federation. 'Sports and alcohol should never be placed together'."[62]

Be that as it may, life as a student athlete is intense. Students who are not involved in athletics probably don't understand how demanding the daily schedule can be for athletes. Training... the need to be competitive and to perform consistently... the stress of maintaining academics and fearing the results if they slip... travel, daily practice, fatigue, rescheduling classes. Time is hard to find. Partying and just hanging out are luxuries athletes can't afford and "catching up" is an ongoing process.

There is, in addition, the stress that comes with the spotlight, the expectation to perform. Athletes are often on display, pushed by coaches, parents and fans to achieve perfection. People applaud when they win and criticize them mercilessly when they fail. In addition to striving to excel athletically, academically, and socially athletes may experience stress due to isolated living conditions in athletic residence halls and long hours spent practicing, training, and traveling. Sometimes the stress builds up. And like a lot of students, athletes find it easier to relieve that stress and to forget about things when they use alcohol or other drugs. Even though they may know they can't be at their best when under "the influence," they take chances. It doesn't matter if you are in the greatest shape of your life, alcohol and other drugs affect an athlete the same way they affect non-athletes.[63]

Research conducted by The College of William and Mary provides insight into some of the deleterious effects alcohol can have on athletic performance:

- Evidence is mounting that even moderate drinking results in a loss of motor coordination 12-18 hours after consumption. Depleted aerobic capacity can last as long as 48 hours after use—many hours after alcohol can no longer be detected in the blood.

- Regular metabolic processes in the liver are interrupted while alcohol is being metabolized. The liver is primarily a producer of glycogen, a basic body fuel. Alcohol metabolism interrupts glycogen production, leading to the depletion of natural glycogen reserves. Thus, alcohol metabolism depletes the body of its natural fuel.

- This glycogen depletion leads directly to an early onset of muscle fatigue during athletic performance. Additionally, without a sufficient glycogen supply, the muscle tissue does not have the energy necessary for cell repair following strenuous exercise.

- Alcohol ingestion and metabolism inhibit functions of the skeletal musculature. Chronic alcohol use causes a progressive weakening of the muscles, both cardiac and skeletal.

Adverse effects of alcohol use that have been seen to last up to 48 hours also include:

- impaired reaction time, balance and eye-hand coordination
- distorted perception, affecting accuracy
- impaired fine motor and gross motor coordination
- decrease in strength
- increased fatigue and decreased aerobic capacity
- difficulty regulating body temperature.[64]

Athletes who cannot handle stress sometimes end up "binge drinking," picking a night to "go crazy" with alcohol or other drugs. Using alcohol to relieve stress usually results in some trouble, little enjoyment and more stress. Alcohol causes you to lose your good judgment, and athletes sometimes overestimate their abilities, doing dangerous stunts or taking unnecessary chances. Athletes need to remember that if they injure themselves at a party because they were drunk, it is still an injury. If they commit a crime while under the influence, it is still a crime.

As an athlete, work hard to manage your time and balance your academic, athletic and personal obligations. When you feel stress building up, look for healthy ways to relax. For some people, that means spending time with supportive friends. For others it is a good workout, extra sleep, time with family or religion. Whatever it is, work it into your schedule before you get stressed out.[65]

> *He used to be such a quiet guy, now his anger is out of control!*
> Bob B. Queens College senior

Steroids

Although steroids do not fall into the category of psychoactive drugs like alcohol or other drugs, I think it's important to add a brief note about them. The pursuit of excellence at any cost sometimes makes steroid use seem attractive. Steroids will contribute to increased muscle strength and bulk but there is usually a serious price to pay for these benefits.

I believe the negative side effects far outweigh any benefits gained by using steroids. The psychological and physical risks include:
- depression and/or aggression;
- if needles are used for injection, sharing needles could lead to HIV or other infections;
- for young men, testicular shrinkage, acne, and loss of hair;
- for young women, irregular menstrual cycle, facial hair, and lower voice;
- damage to the growth area of the bones resulting in a permanent stunting of growth;
- weakening of tendons resulting in tearing and rupture.

There is one other concern with steroid use. An athlete with a positive result from a drug test for steroids will face possible suspension or dismissal from his/her respective team.

Here are a few guidelines that may help you maintain your mental and physical health while performing at an optimal level:
- develop an effective time management plan for balancing studies, practice, work and social time;
- maintain a healthy diet;
- take advantage of campus support services;

- sleep whenever possible;
- attend classes regularly;
- practice healthy stress reduction exercises such as meditation or prayer;
- socialize with your non-athlete peers as well as teammates;
- take extra special care when making decisions about alcohol or other drug use.

♦

Chapter Eleven

Spring Break

... a good time is had by all,

maybe.

"So spring break is coming up—endless hangovers, unwanted calories, spending money and so many other risks. Actually, I guess spring break is a very dangerous ritual."

Karen P., University of Massachusetts junior

"The bars don't care who's drinking as long as they're making money. My freshman year I got into every Florida bar and I didn't even have a fake ID. I didn't need it. At one of the bars the bouncer told my girlfriend that if she lifted her blouse for him, he'd let her in."

Jessica F., Massachusetts Institute of Technology senior

"It's a damn good excuse to drink and party for ten days straight and not feel guilty about it (not that guilty anyway)."

Anonymous

"I've been to Italy, Greece, and England in the past three years. I've traveled and seen more and spent less than my friends who have gone to Florida to get drunk! Why don't they just stay home and buy a sunlamp and a keg?"

Allison F., Keene State College junior

Spring Break

RESPONDING TO CLEAR AND PERSISTENT public criticism leveled at spring break excesses and at the beer industry's role on students' annual excursions south, breweries have pulled back from sponsoring spring break activities. Missing in 1992 were Miller's "How to Scam Babes" and "Starting Spring Training Early."[66] Nonetheless, there was little reduction in alcohol consumption during spring break 1992. Legal-age drinkers reported consuming an average of ten beers per night during spring break.[67] Today, this dangerous ritual continues and is perpetuated by high profile media coverage.

Spring break is a college ritual long associated with excessive alcohol or other drug use. But at what cost? Researchers found that the daily consumption of five to nine drinks per day (at a rate that kept the BAL lower than .08) for just eight days by non-alcoholic subjects resulted in some signs of liver damage.[68] How much damage is taking place in Florida, the Caribbean, and Mexico during spring break? Please remember, if you choose to consume alcohol during spring break, the possible injuries, trauma or sexually transmitted diseases that could occur will follow you home no matter how far away you traveled.

When traveling to some exotic foreign land, high risk alcohol consumption, illegal drug use and/or rowdy behavior can have some devastating results. When traveling abroad remember that a drug that may be legal in one country could be illegal in another. Behavior that may be legal in the United States could be illegal in another country. Being an American does not excuse any disruptive or illegal behavior in a foreign land. As a matter of fact, in some countries you could become a target for the local police officials *because* you are an American. Being arrested in a foreign land can be a scary, dangerous experience. You can avoid turning your wonderful spring break into a horrible memory by avoiding high risk drinking or other drug use, avoiding rowdy behavior and familiarizing yourself with the laws and customs of the country you are visiting before you leave on your trip.

The notorious saloon owner and judge, Roy Bean had his saloon situated next to the railroad station. Trains stopped there twice daily for ten minutes. The parched passengers usually availed themselves of the occasion to get a drink at the judge's place. Bean never gave one of these customers change. He always delayed matters until the whistle blew and the train was about to pull out, forcing the travelers to hot foot it to the station if they did not want to miss the train and be stranded in the middle of nowhere.

Many colleges and universities are now offering Alternative Spring Break programs such as working in a third-world country, building a house for a needy family, or participating in an archaeological dig. More specifically, here are examples of some campus Alternative Spring Break programs. In 1998 students from Cornell University assisted with repairs and child care at a domestic abuse shelter in West Virginia. Students from Jacksonville University worked with the homeless in a number of Florida communities in 1999. Also in that same year, Keene State College conducted three Habitat for Humanity programs around the United States and Wilkes University students worked with children in Tijuanna, Mexico. Speak to your campus community service coordinator about what is available through your institution.

If your campus does not conduct an Alternative Spring Break program, contact Break Away or any of the other opportunities listed in the "Resources" section of this book. These organizations provide information regarding program planning and volunteer placement with both national and international community organizations. If you're more inclined, try a recreational break that includes white-water rafting, mountain climbing or bicycle touring. ◆

Chapter Twelve

Advertising

... this Bud's for you.

"The sellers of alcohol should have the right to advertise their product. But, they should be considerate of who is most likely going to be seeing their ads and who will be influenced."
Johnson L., Michigan State University senior

"They do have a right to advertise since it's a legal drug. We need to educate people about the lies they are selling."
Allison T., Fordham University junior

Advertising

UPON YOUR ARRIVAL on the college campus, you became a major target of the alcohol advertising industry. Sponsorships and promotions on college campuses by alcohol producers and the use of celebrities and youth-oriented musical groups in advertising create a pro-use drinking environment.[69] The alcohol industry is counting on you to fuel their sales. After all, they keep killing off their older customers, so they need new ones. The college campus provides fertile ground for new ones:

- "The alcohol industry spends $23 million annually for on-campus promotion, principally for beer advertising."[70] Beer and alcohol advertisers are the source of one third of all college newspaper revenue.[71]

- "U.S. college students will spend $5.5 billion on alcohol."[72]

- "The 'college scene' is where 5 percent of the American population is estimated to generate 10 percent of all brewers' revenues."[73]

- "This translates into $1 billion in college sales for Anheuser-Busch and $353 million for Miller Brewing."[74] It is interesting to note here that approximately 76% of all excessive (five or more drinks in a day) alcohol consumption is beer and that 49% of beer drinkers drink excessively.

- On average, college student spend more money on booze than books. Most college students drink more beer than anything else.[75]

"Often peer pressure is cited as the primary cause of high risk alcohol consumption on the college campus. But what influences these peers? How are they socialized? The industry's own advertising relies heavily on peer pressure. The rock stars, celebrities and athletes who frolic in the beer commercials serve as 'sample peers'

In the Old West, the sign over a Georgetown, Colorado saloon for a long time bore the legend, "We serve the WORST liquor," a joke played on the illiterate owner by an underpaid sign painter. It brought in so many customers that the saloon keeper left it hanging even after he found out what it meant.

promoting drinking as an integral part of collegiate life. Beer advertising provides an entry level education for youth about the uses and gratification of the product. Positive images consistently link desirable traits to their product and reinforce the association."[76]

If you are an average 18- or 19-year-old entering college, you have been viewing nearly one thousand beer, wine and liquor ads in the mass media each year. This advertising promotes the perceived benefits of alcohol consumption. Take a good look at the advertisements for alcohol. Are the images they present consistent with what you view on your campus? Or, are there many more negative outcomes than the industry would like to let you know? Is the portrayal of women in these ads consistent with your beliefs? If not, do you realize that by purchasing these products you are perpetuating the myths they present about alcohol consumption and women?

If you are disturbed by the images presented in alcohol advertising, then I have a suggestion. Have you ever noticed that in every magazine you pick up, there's a bunch of postcards urging you to subscribe to the magazine? Well, send in the card letting the publisher know you would consider subscribing if they would remove the degrading and misleading ads for alcohol. It will cost you nothing if you use their cards. And, you will be making an important statement regarding the portrayal of women in advertising as well as your desire for truth in advertising.   ◆

Advertising

Personal Challenge: Drinking Choices

Goal:
To raise awareness of the factors that may influence your drinking choices

Instructions:
Circle the answer that best reflects the degree to which the situation influences you to want to have a drink

1. You were eating an enjoyable meal?
Definitely Yes   Probably Yes   Maybe   Probably No   Definitely No

2. You were watching television?
Definitely Yes   Probably Yes   Maybe   Probably No   Definitely No

3. You were visiting friends, some of whom were drinking?
Definitely Yes   Probably Yes   Maybe   Probably No   Definitely No

4. You had just completed a difficult task that had taken you a long time to finish?
Definitely Yes   Probably Yes   Maybe   Probably No   Definitely No

5. You were tense and anxious?
Definitely Yes   Probably Yes   Maybe   Probably No   Definitely No

6. You just had a big argument with someone in your family?
Definitely Yes   Probably Yes   Maybe   Probably No   Definitely No

7. You were relaxing after a busy day?
Definitely Yes   Probably Yes   Maybe   Probably No   Definitely No

8. You hadn't had a drink in awhile and someone offered you one?
Definitely Yes   Probably Yes   Maybe   Probably No   Definitely No

9. You were waiting for a very important phone call that was 15 minutes late?
Definitely Yes   Probably Yes   Maybe   Probably No   Definitely No

10. You were at a party and someone offered you a drink?
Definitely Yes   Probably Yes   Maybe   Probably No   Definitely No

11. You were at a sporting or entertainment event?

Definitely Yes   Probably Yes   Maybe   Probably No   Definitely No

12. You felt as if you really needed a drink?

Definitely Yes   Probably Yes   Maybe   Probably No   Definitely No

13. You were with a friend who urged you to drink?

Definitely Yes   Probably Yes   Maybe   Probably No   Definitely No

14. You were meeting a few friends in a bar?

Definitely Yes   Probably Yes   Maybe   Probably No   Definitely No

15. You were alone and feeling depressed?

Definitely Yes   Probably Yes   Maybe   Probably No   Definitely No

16. You were celebrating a special occasion?

Definitely Yes   Probably Yes   Maybe   Probably No   Definitely No

17. You were doing paperwork such as studying, paying bills, or writing a letter?

Definitely Yes   Probably Yes   Maybe   Probably No   Definitely No

18. You wanted to feel more sophisticated and attractive?

Definitely Yes   Probably Yes   Maybe   Probably No   Definitely No

19. You were bored?

Definitely Yes   Probably Yes   Maybe   Probably No   Definitely No

20. Could you refrain from drinking regardless of the circumstances?

Definitely Yes   Probably Yes   Maybe   Probably No   Definitely No

Scoring for this exercise can be found in the Challenge Results Section at the end of the book.

Reflections:

a. What factors influence your drinking choices?

b. For each of the statements you answered "Yes", are there other ways to deal with the situation rather than drinking alcohol?

Adapted from Making Choices: A Personal Look at Alcohol & Drug Use (1992). McGraw-Hill Higher Education, Quinn/Scaffa

13

Other Drugs

... alcohol is not the only danger.

"To tell you the truth, I don't understand why more people don't smoke pot."

Anonymous

"Pot had a strange effect on me. I viewed life through a checker-board, able to see only through the white squares. While stoned I only saw pieces of life. But then I started to feel that way even when I wasn't loaded. I realized this is not how I wanted to experience life."

Anonymous

"Sure there are some benefits from the hemp plant, but I wouldn't want to get in a car with someone who just smoked a joint nor would I want to be on the same road with another driver who just had a couple of hits on a bong."

Ann D., Michigan State University senior

Other Drugs

OBVIOUSLY, THIS BOOK IS ABOUT ALCOHOL because, when it comes to socializing, it is the drug of choice for most college students. Just like drinking, a common misperception about other drug use is that most students use some type of illegal drug. Yet, all the research available indicates that the use of drugs other than alcohol on the college campus is done by a minority of students. The fact of the matter is that most students do not use illegal drugs and most of the students who do use them, do so only occasionally. Once again, in addition to numerous other research projects, the results of the 1998 Core Survey can shed some interesting light on the reality of illegal drug use. The number of students who reported using marijuana at least once during the year prior to the survey was 32 percent and cocaine use during the prior year was reported by 5 percent of students. The number of students who reported using marijuana at least once during the month prior to the survey was 19 percent and cocaine use during the prior month was reported by 2 percent of students.[77]

One of the primary reasons why many people believe that the majority of students use drugs other than alcohol at a high risk level is that just like high risk drinking, the use of other drugs has a very high profile on the campus. Illegal drug use and all the surrounding complications create very spicy headlines. As a result, the newspaper coverage then raises the profile of these users, thus contributing to the misperception that many college students are using. Please do not let this high profile trick you into believing that everyone uses drugs.

In the first edition of <u>Beer, Booze and Books</u> I included a very brief chapter on the other drugs. The response by many of the readers was, "Jim, you need to have more about the other drugs in your next book." In meeting the suggestions of those students, I have now included a brief overview of many of the more popular drugs used by some college students. I hesitate to offer more than this brief overview due to the broad scope of the issues that need to be addressed. Hundreds of books are available regarding drugs and their unique qualities and dangers. Once again, let me refer you to Buzzed[78] one of the best books available for information regarding the pharmacological, psychological and emotional concerns we have for drug use. For the moment however, here are some of the popular drugs and the pertinent information about their use

Cocaine

Type of Drug: Cocaine is a central nervous system stimulant.

Historical Perspective: Processed cocaine is derived from the leaves of the cocoa shrub which is generally found in the mountainous regions of Central and South America. In leaf form it has been used for centuries by the indigenous people of that area as a mild stimulant and tonic for dealing with the rigors of mountain living.

Addiction Potential: High to extreme depending on the form and method of delivery. The intensity of the high as well as the immediate and extreme withdrawal following use, especially if smoked, contribute to the extreme addictive nature of cocaine.

Method of Delivery: Cocaine can be inhaled, smoked or injected depending on the form in which it is used. It can also be used, although rarely, intravenously.

Medicinal Use: Many people in Central and South America chew the leaves of the cocoa plant for its mild stimulating effects. It is also used by inhabitants of the mountains as a medicinal elixir to relieve the debilitating effects of altitude. Since it will cause a numbing effect when inhaled and acts as a vasoconstrictor, it can also be used by surgeons for nasal and throat surgery.

Acute Effects: Once ingested, usually by either sniffing or smoking, cocaine will create a mild feeling of euphoria accompanied by an increase in the user's heartbeat, rate of breathing, and blood pressure creating a perceived energy surge and alertness. Other physical symptoms include an increase in core body temperature, sweating, dilated pupils and pallor. It decreases the appetite of the user while also increasing blood sugar. Heavier dosages could lead to violent, bizarre and erratic behavior

Short Term Dangers: Cocaine will contribute to irritability, restlessness, and sleeplessness. It can also cause a seizure, heart attack or stroke with just one dose. And, this dose does not need to be an overdose to be deadly! Some users combine alcohol or depressant drugs to mitigate some of the extreme restlessness caused by cocaine. This combination can also cause severe and possibly fatal reactions.

Effects of Long Term Use: Initially, frequent users will develop prolonged coldlike symptoms. Over a longer period of time, if inhaled regularly, cocaine can contribute to erosion of the nasal septum. Heavy users who sniff the drug have been known to develop an actual hole in their septum. Since it is an appetite suppressant, frequent users and addicts often suffer from malnutrition. Long term cocaine users and addicts usually suffer from many of the same problems that those addicted to other drugs experience including, severe psychological, social, biological and financial problems,

Other Concerns: Sexual problems can develop including erectile dysfunction, low sperm count and male infertility. As with any drug available on the street, you never know the exact strength of the dosage used. One time it may contain a high degree of additives and be about 50 percent pure. Another time it could be 95 percent pure and extremely deadly. Also, procaine, benzocaine or amphetamine may be used as additives or substitutes thereby contributing to further dangers.

Ecstasy

Type of Drug: Ecstasy is unique in that it is both a stimulant and an hallucinogen. This combination is what makes it so appealing and yet so dangerous.

Historical Perspective: Relatively speaking, ecstasy is new to the drug scene. It was originally developed as an appetite suppressant in the 1930s, however, recreational use did not emerge until the 1960s and 1970s. The misperception of ecstasy as a so-called "safe" drug has contributed to a dramatic increase in ecstasy use in the 1990s and will probably continue until prevention specialists are able to convince the public of the extreme dangers associated with this drug.

Addiction Potential: The potential for physical addiction to ecstasy is moderate.

Method of Delivery: Ecstasy is usually taken orally.

Medicinal Use: Due to its ability to increase empathic feelings in the user, it had originally been used in therapy, in particular, couples therapy. I believe, along with most professionals in the alcohol and other drug field, the potential psychological, emotional and physical dangers involved in the use of this drug far outweigh any therapeutic value.

Acute Effects: The euphoric feelings generated by this drug are usually accompanied by mild hallucinations. It is referred to as the "love drug" or the "hug drug" due to the increased empathy and the enhanced sensuality that it creates. Some users report increased stimulation while others report a mild relaxation effect.

Short Term Dangers: Some of the more uncomfortable effects include dilated pupils, nausea, muscle tension and grinding teeth. One of the most serious dangers resulting from the use of ecstasy is dehydration. This acute dehydration can cause kidney failure and possible death. Since it is a stimulant, the increased heart rate could also be deadly for those with heart problems. Unlike many of the other drugs, ecstasy can cause brain damage with just one use however the damage done is not noticeable initially.

Effects of Long Term Use: Many users believe, or should I say want to believe, that ecstasy is not dangerous. It is hard for them to believe that something that could make us feel so good could be so dangerous. The most current research reveals that this is an extremely dangerous drug. Although uncommon, not only can ecstacy kill someone with the very first use, but brain damage can occur with just one use or over a period of time and occasional use. Researchers now believe that continued exposure to ecstasy destroys the brain cells responsible for providing us with feelings of pleasure. So, although this drug can provide an intense short term pleasurable feeling, overtime, we may be able to generate only limited feelings of pleasure without the assistance of some drug.

Other Concerns: As indicated, this drug is known for its ability to increase sensuality. However, the interesting irony is that, if in fact a sexual encounter does develop, ecstasy will most likely contribute to sexual dysfunction. Male users may not be able to achieve an erection and, if they are capable, ecstasy can easily cause an inability to ejaculate. Female users experience greater difficulty in achieving an orgasm. Dentists report a growing concern for the dental health of users. The grinding effect produced by the drug has many users wearing away the enamel on their teeth resulting in serious tooth decay. One other concern is the fact that ecstasy is usually made by non-professionals. As with many street drugs, you never quite know the exact dosage you are taking nor do you know what other ingredients have been included or excluded. An inaccurately mixed dosage has been seen to produce Parkinson's Disease-like symptoms in some users.

GHB (Gamma Hydroxybutyric Acid)

Type of Drug: Sedative

Historical Perspective: Along with Rohypnol, GHB is sold in foreign countries as an aid to sleep disorders. It had been sold in health food stores in the United States in the 1980s as an alternative to steroids but as the number of people dying due to its use rose, the federal government banned it in 1990.

Addiction Potential: The addiction potential for GHB is not currently known however, since it is a sedative drug, for the regular user tolerance and withdrawal are probable.

Method of Delivery: Clear, somewhat salty liquid usually mixed with a drink.

Medicinal Use: GHB has been used in foreign countries for treatment of sleep disorders, narcolepsy and alcoholism. It has also been used as a surgical anesthetic.

Acute Effects: GHB produces a number of effects similar to Rohypnol including mild euphoria, nausea and dizziness. This can be combined with memory loss and/or loss of consciousness. When combined with other drugs such as cocaine or alcohol its effects can be extremely dangerous and deadly.

Short Term Dangers: GHB can slow down the central nervous system so much so that the user can become comatose. Most users come out of the coma but some still remain in a coma today. Others have died.

Long Term Effects: Presently there is little known about the long term effects. Given that it is a sedative drug, the long term effects are probably similar to, if not more toxic, than other sedative drugs.

Other Concerns: Because GHB can be manufactured on a kitchen stove with ingredients readily available (mixture of chemicals normally used in cleaning fluids such as lye), users can never be sure of the dosage or the actual ingredients. The mild taste makes it easy to place in a drink without the drinker knowing it.

Heroin

Type of Drug: Heroin is an opiate derived from opium which is a product of the poppy plant. (The painkillers morphine and codeine are also opiates.)

Historical Perspective: The use of opiates as a pain killer and for other medicinal purposes, dates back to prehistoric times. Heroin was first synthesized from morphine and was originally considered to be non-addictive in the late 1800s. Shortly after its development, the true addictive nature of this drug was realized. In 1914, the Harrison Act established licensing procedures for medicinal opiate use and non-medicinal use was banned.

Addiction Potential: Extreme. Although withdrawal from heroin addiction is extremely painful and debilitating, it is not deadly like the withdrawal from addiction to depressant drugs such as alcohol.

Method of Delivery: In the past heroin was usually injected. Recently snorting heroin has become more popular probably due to the increased level of purity and/or perhaps as a result of fear of AIDS due to the use of infected needles. Smoking, also known as "chasing the dragon," was popular in the opium dens of the late 1800s and continues today.

Medicinal Use: Heroin and its precursor morphine have been used as effective pain killers.

Acute Effects: Heroin injectors describe it as a rush of pleasure and a wave of relaxation. It creates an intense euphoric, dream-like state in the user followed by drowsiness and sedation. Pain is also relieved by heroin.

Short Term Dangers: The primary concerns for the user are similar to those concerns for anyone using street drugs: lack of consistency in dosage and lack of purity both potentially resulting in a deadly overdose. Overdosing can cause respiratory depression, cardiac arrest, shock, coma or death. There is also the danger of an allergic reaction to substances used to dilute the drug. Vomiting and constipation often accompany heroin use.

Effects of Long Term Use: Dependency can develop within just a few weeks of daily use. Men may suffer from a number of different sexual dysfunctions and women often cease having menstrual cycles. Constipation and malnutrition are also seen in long term users. Long term users may also suffer from brain damage due to decreased levels of oxygen in the blood (hypoxia). Surprisingly, although many health problems do arise for the heroin user due to his/her lifestyle choices, damage to the rest of the body specifically caused by heroin is somewhat negligible.

Other Concerns: The risk of AIDS and other infectious diseases is extreme when addicts share needles.

LSD (Lysergic Acid Diethylamide)

Type of Drug Hallucinogen

Historical Perspective: LSD was originally synthesized in the 1940s however hallucinogen use dates back to prehistoric times. LSD use was most extreme in the late 1960s and into the 1970s. Contrary to media reports about LSD's loss of popularity, it remains one of the most commonly used hallucinogens today.

Addiction Potential: Low. Physical addiction is highly unlikely but psychological dependence is easily developed.

Method of Delivery: LSD is taken orally via sugar pills, blotter paper or small gelatin pieces. It can also be ingested via teas or broths.

Medicinal Use: LSD has had limited use in mental hospitals and laboratories to study mental disorders.

Acute Effects: The user's personality, experience with drugs, expectations and mood will trigger a variety of responses to LSD and other hallucinogens. The setting in which they are taken and the people surrounding the user will also have a dramatic impact on the acute effects of these drugs. As the name suggests it induces hallucinations along with a distortion of time and space perception as well as sensations of disconnectedness with reality. Other acute effects include blurred vision, visual patterns, feelings of increased personal insight and expansion of consciousness.

Short Term Dangers: With the exception of possible acute anxiety reactions, LSD does not seem to cause dangerous physical reactions. However, any hallucinogenic experience can produce anxiety, paranoia or severe panic. Also, hallucinogens sometimes add to an existing neurosis or character disorder. Although uncommon, psychotic reactions can occur.

Effects of Long Term Use: Flashbacks (experiencing hallucinations and other visual disturbances in the absence of the drug) are fairly common in heavy LSD users. Other visual disturbances experienced by the long term user indicate the possibility of brain damage that will persist long after the cessation of use.

Other Concerns: There are a number of other hallucinogens including psilocybin mushrooms, Phencyclidine (PCP), Ketamine (Special K), mescaline and mescaline-like drugs. These drugs place the user at risk for a number of adverse reactions and dangers. Some of these reactions and/or dangers are milder than those caused by LSD use while others are much more serious, including death.

Marijuana

Type of Drug: Hallucinogen/Narcotic

Historical Perspective: Marijuana comes from the cannabis plant which has both psychoactive properties and medicinal value as well as industrial applications. Concrete evidence of marijuana use in China for its psychoactive properties dates back to the first century BC and there is evidence that it was probably even earlier. Evidence also suggests there was use of marijuana during this time in Europe and Egypt as well.

Addiction Potential: Low. (Much controversy surrounds the question of marijuana's addiction potential. Users can certainly develop a psychological dependence on marijuana. Current research suggests that heavy users may also experience symptoms of physical withdrawal in the absence of the drug indicating physical addiction. However, these symptoms of withdrawal are not as profound as withdrawal from other drugs such as heroin or alcohol.)

Method of Delivery: Marijuana is usually smoked. It can be mixed with other ingredients then cooked and eaten.

Medicinal Use: Delta-9-tetrahydrocannabinol (THC), the primary psychoactive metabolite that is present in the bloodstream following the ingestion of marijuana has unique pharmacological actions and numerous medicinal uses. It can be used as an anti-nausea agent for cancer patients utilizing chemotherapy. It can help relieve the introcular pressure in the eye due to glaucoma. There are other drugs that deliver these same benefits without the negative side effects of smoking marijuana such as its psychoactive properties and the noxious chemicals also present in marijuana smoke. Scientists are currently attempting to develop efficient delivery methods which will not subject the patients to those negative side effects. Other medicinal uses are currently under investigation.

Acute Effects: More so than most other drugs, the acute effects of marijuana are significantly impacted by the environment. Users may shift from extreme laughter to quiet introspection. Some people are stimulated by marijuana while others are sedated. The same people may experience different effects at different times based on the quality of the marijuana, the amount of the dose and the people surrounding the user. High grade marijuana with elevated THC content and hashish (made from the resin of the plant) can produce hallucinations. Other effects could include time distortion and paranoia.

Short Term Dangers: Due to the nature of the drug, overdose is virtually impossible. However, injuries and death can occur due to poor judgment, lack of coordination and other impairment complications. Contrary to what many students claim, users do not drive better when stoned. Research indicates the greater the THC level in the blood, the greater the impairment of driving ability.

Long Term Effects: There are numerous negative effects resulting from long term use of marijuana. However, the "marijuana trap" is that the nature of these undesirable negative effects often renders these effects unnoticeable by the user. It is only after the cessation of use that the smoker notices how the marijuana had been impacting his/her performance. Some of the more profound problems include:
- deficits in attention and recall
- impairment in the ability to shift attention
- deficits in verbal IQ and verbal learning
- diminished ability to respond to unique complex tasks
- inability to reject irrelevant sensory input
- impairment of short term memory

Even though many of the effects of long term use may be reversible after a period of abstinence and there is no evidence of gross organic change to the brain structure, marijuana use can have a significant negative impact on the success of regular users. Yes, just like alcohol use, there are those who can use heavily and be successful, more often than not however, the regular marijuana user does not meet his/her true academic potential and level of success.

The smoker is subjecting her/himself to numerous noxious and carcinogenic chemicals including benzopyrene, carbon monoxide, hydrogen cyanide and tar when smoking. The presence of these carcinogens in the marijuana smoke suggests a greater risk for cancer in heavy smokers. Currently, there seems to be no epidemiological evidence of an increase in other diseases due to marijuana use other than respiratory disease. Debate continues regarding the impact of marijuana on the immune system.

Other Concerns: The nature of this book limits a comprehensive look at marijuana. As you can see by the above information, marijuana remains a very controversial drug. Although the occasional use of marijuana by fully developed adults has minimal negative effects beyond the increased risks for impairment problems, marijuana use can have a significant negative impact on the physical, emotional and social development of teens and young adults.

Nitrous Oxide

Type of Drug: It is difficult to categorize nitrous oxide. It can best be described as an anesthetic.

Historical Perspective: Also known as laughing gas, nitrous oxide has been abused to produce a high for more than one hundred years. At least one nineteenth century scientist reported his own use of nitrous to achieve its psychedelic effects.

Addiction Potential: Low

Method of Delivery: Nitrous oxide is a colorless gas that is inhaled from pressurized tanks or capsules. When used medicinally, it is mixed with oxygen and has a concentration of 60-80% nitrous oxide.

Medicinal Use: It is used medically to produce a mild but clinically useful level of anesthesia. It is primarily used by dentists. It is also used as a prelude for a variety of medical procedures.

Acute Effects: The high from nitrous oxide lasts very briefly, and dissipates approximately five minutes after acute inhalation. It produces feelings of euphoria and a dream like state. Additionally nitrous oxide may produce a floating feeling or a "coasting" sensation. Some people experience negative feelings of uneasiness and anxiety.

Short Term Dangers: The intoxication from nitrous oxide can contribute to unconsciousness, memory loss and psychomotor impairment, resulting in injuries due to accidents. Nitrous oxide can cause damage to the tissue it comes in contact with including the mouth, trachea and lungs.

Long Term Effects: Chronic use of nitrous oxide can contribute to a decrease in the production of both red and white blood cells. This could lead to anemia and a possible increased risk for infection. This could also exaggerate any pre-existing immune system problem. Finally, regular users with emphysema or asthma risk a severe decrease in blood oxygen level which could have a disastrous result.

Rohypnol

Type of Drug: Sedative in the benzodiazepine family (Valium, librium and xanax are also benzodiazepines.)

Historical Perspective: Even though it is manufactured and used in Europe, the Asian Pacific and Latin America, the manufacturers of Rohypnol, Hoffman LaRoche, have never sought approval for its use in the United States. It is not marketed legally in the United States but is commonly imported illegally through Mexico and South America where it is legal.

Addiction Potential: As with most sedative drugs rohypnol has a moderate to high addiction potential.

Method of Delivery: Rohypnol is usually taken orally in pill form.

Other Drugs

Medicinal Use: Rohypnol is prescribed by physicians overseas for people with sleeping disorders.

Acute Effects: Rohypnol intoxication is generally associated with impaired judgment and motor skills, loss of inhibitions and slowed heartbeat. When mixed with alcohol, narcotic drugs or any other central nervous system depressant, the results can be life-threatening and fatal. Perpetrators of sexual assault find this drug particularly effective because it can cause extended memory loss (8-24 hours) especially when used in high dosages or when mixed with alcohol.

Short Term Dangers: "Blackouts" are a serious concern with the use of Rohypnol. The loss of inhibitions are of major concern as well.

Effects of Long Term Use: Like other sedative-hypnotics, rohypnol can produce physical dependence. An abrupt cessation of use can cause anxiety, depression, insomnia, intense dreaming, intense sensitivity to light and sounds, possible seizure and possibly death.

Other Concerns: Because the older form of rohypnol was odorless, colorless and tasteless, it could easily be slipped into someone's drink without their knowledge. These qualities of rohypnol have fostered its use in "acquaintance rapes." As a result, the manufacturers are now producing it so that when placed in a drink, it will turn the drink blue. ◆

14

Get Involved

... contributing to a safe and healthy community.

I was in SADD in high school and wanted to do that kind of thing in college too.

Janet, University of Massachusetts first-year student

I don't care what they say or do to us, we are going to drink no matter what!

Ralph R., Michigan State University junior

It all seems so hopeless.

Jason M., University of Pittsburgh junior

After her death I decided to try to make a change on my campus. I have enjoyed the challenges so much that I am now getting my degree in counseling. I hope to be able to work on a college campus in the future and help students avoid alcohol problems.

Angel B., University of Colorado senior

Get Involved

A S A COLLEGE STUDENT YOU HAVE BECOME A MEMBER OF A COMMUNITY that can use your help. And, the high risk use of alcohol and the other drugs can create serious problems in your campus community. As you have seen in this book, these problems can have a dramatic impact on not only your own life but the lives of everyone around you. You can help in reducing these problems. How you help is up to you. But, the value of your contribution cannot be underestimated.

Why bother?

Extensive research indicates that abstainers and low risk drinkers experience widespread harm resulting from others' misuse of alcohol. Secondary binge effects can range from interrupted study and sleep to destruction of property, assault, and unwanted sexual advances. Here's just one example of a "secondary binge effect." You spend the evening out with a friend including dinner, a movie, maybe even a drink or two. The evening comes to an end and you head back to your residence hall. Upon your arrival to your room you see your roommate asleep in your bed. This may not disturb you so you choose to sleep in your roommate's bed. Then you find out why your roommate is in your bed. Your roommate moved to your bed because she had vomited in her own bed.

The secondary effects of binge drinking jeopardize the collegial and scholarly environment that university administrators and faculty hope to create for their students. Some might argue that most heavy drinkers, if left alone, will eventually learn from the adverse consequences of their drinking and, as they mature, will approach alcohol consumption with a greater sense of responsibility. This is not always true, and in the meantime, other students, both non-bingers and those who abstain, are left to fend for themselves against the inconsiderate, insulting, intimidating, and sometimes criminal behavior of their binge drinking classmates. On campuses where high risk drinking (also referred to as binge drinking) is done by more than half the students, fully 87 percent of the non-binge drinkers who lived in dormitories, fraternities, or sororities experienced one or more negative consequences caused by the excessive drinking by other students. And, the grades of non-drinkers may also be impacted negatively since on these same campuses 70% of the students report having their studying or sleep interrupted by drinkers. even on low drinking-level campuses, with 35 percent or fewer students classified as binge drinkers, a substantial majority, 62 percent, also reported experiencing such consequences.[79] In other words, on campuses, the heavier the drinking the more students – even non-drinking or low risk drinking students – are negatively affercted by alcohol. Therefore, contributing to the education and abuse prevention efforts on your campus has the potential for improving the lives of not only the high risk drinkers themselves but also everyone being impacted by the excessive drinking of others.

> *The best thing I can do is live a healthy life and be a role model for*
> *new students.*
>
> John R., Keene State College senior

Imaginary Peers

Throughout this book you have been reading a number of stories and some statistics that seem to indicate the majority of students are drinking and having problems as a result of that consumption. However, I have also tried to reinforce the fact that choosing to abstain from alcohol or drink alcohol at a low risk level is really not unusual. Despite all the aforementioned tragedies occurring in the lives of many students, ongoing research indicates 17 percent of college students do not drink, 18 percent drink between one and six times per year, 42 percent drink between one and four times per month and yet only24 percent drink three or more times per week. Reports on other drinking patterns also indicate that a majority of students drink at a low risk level: 48 percent of college students average either none or one drink per week and 29 percent average between two and nine drinks per week.[80] (Nine drinks per week could be low risk depending upon the age and gender of the drinker as well as how many are consumed in one sitting.)

It is common for many students, especially students who drink heavilty, to dismiss these survey results as misrepresentations or outright lies by the survey respondents. Without going into the details of how the validity of these numerous surveys is established, let me assure you, the results are reliable. Even if there are some discrepancies in the results, the bottom line is only a minority of students around the country drink at a high risk level—yes a high profile minority—but a minority nonetheless. How do we come to believe that "everyone" is abusing alcohol when the data suggests large numbers are either abstaining or consuming at a low risk level? Some possible factors include:

- The intoxicated student makes a vivid impression by being loud, aggressive, obnoxious or promiscuous.
- Observers, especially when drinking, do not notice their less obvious, non-using peers but rather tend to observe other drinkers.
- Non-drinkers and low risk drinkers are not as likely to gather in large, obvious groups or settings such as alcohol-related parties.
- People who are having a good time at a party and abstaining or drinking minimally could appear to be drinking excessively.
- Typical conversations focus on excessive alcohol use and little conversation portrays restraint in any positive light. (People who abstain or drink minimally are not very likely to say something like "I had a blast at that party. It was great and a lot of us didn't drink any booze.")[81]

In summary, "the abuse of alcohol in student groups and social settings may be recalled more vividly and quickly than actions surrounding abstinence or moderation, thereby getting a disproportionate amount of attention in peer conversation as well as in mass media news and popular entertainment images. The inordinate public attention and peer talk about the antics of intoxicated peers and campus drinking events may inflate a student's sense of what is normal or typical behavior among peers. Athletes or fraternity and sorority affiliates may have higher levels of alcohol use than the campuswide average at some institutions and, simultaneously, may have greater visibility in the campus culture than most other students, potentially further distorting perceptions of what is characteristic of most students."[82]

One of the most interesting challenges professionals face today in educating students about this issue is understanding the reality that most college students either do not drink or if they do, they do so at a low risk level. Why is it important that we reduce the misperception that most students are high risk drinkers? Well, consider this. National, regional and campus surveys of college students indicate that many students greatly overestimate the amount of high-risk drinking that occurs on college campuses. Based on this misperception, some students may conclude that high-risk drinking is the social norm. This in turn could lead students to increase their own alcohol consumptionin in an attempt to participate in what they imagine is normal drinking. In other words, the misperception may cause students to believe they are both justified and pressured to consume large amounts of alcohol in order to be like other students - their imaginary peers.

Contributing

Each individual on your campus is responsible *for* his or her own choices. However, we can all be responsible *to* each other as well. If you are concerned about the health and safety of your peers, there are a number of opportunities for you to be a contributing member of your campus community. In his book <u>The Education of Character,</u> Dr. Will Keim says it best when it comes to getting involved. "Contributors are men and women of character who are open to the ideas of others. They search for better ways to do things, never say 'never' and are teachable people who are willing to learn. Contributors are responsible and imaginative and work for the betterment of all concerned. They utilize existing resources and solicit new ones. Contributors treat other people as they would like to be treated and 'own their own evaluations' of others. They are respected because they respect others and are good stewards of themselves and their organizations. Contributors develop a good sense of humor and laugh with others, not at them. Contributors admit mistakes and are patient with themselves and others. They are men and women of integrity who say what they mean and do what they say."[83]

Most campuses have an administrator, staff member or committee responsible for the development and implementation of alcohol and other drug education and abuse prevention programs. Consult with them to find out what you can do. I am sure they will welcome your energy, dedication and contribution to these programs. Here are some ways you can help:
- Participate in peer outreach programs.
- Help develop Alcohol Awareness Week if your campus conducts such an event.
- Assist residential life staff in developing educational and social programs.
- Support social events conducted by your Student Activities Department.
- If you join a campus organization, be sure the members understand their responsibility for conducting social events and follow appropriate party management guidelines.
- Participate in discussions about campus alcohol and other drug policies with campus leaders.
- Work with campus administrators and committees in reducing the role of alcohol in the campus environment. ◆

Get Involved

Personal Challenge: Your Contribution

Goal:

To identify ways you can set an example and be a contributor to the individuals and groups with whom you interact on a daily basis.

Instructions:

Making a contribution means setting the example for others. Make a list describing how you can make a contribution to the following groups:
a. your friends
b. your living group
c. your campus
d. your local community

Reflections:

a. Have you ever previously thought of yourself as a contributor to your friends, living group, college or local community? Is this a comfortable role in which to see yourself? Why or why not?
b. How do you think people's words and actions might be different if everyone thought of themselves as contributors?
c. Are you aware of an experience where you have set the example for your friends or another group? What was that experience like for you?

Adapted from Activities Manual for The Education of Character, Lessons for Beginners, Will Keim (1995). Harcourt Brace College Publishers

Chapter Fifteen

Success

... it's up to you.

"If students started to realize they have to please themselves in order to be happy then their lives would be so much more fulfill ing. We take into account too much of other people's views and beliefs. We live by them instead of living by our own values and it's really rather sad."

Jim K., University of Vermont sophomore

"I've started taking road trips on the weekends for the sole reason of getting away from the party scene. It's just become so boring and monotonous. I'm sick of coming home drunk every Friday and Saturday night and waking up the next morning hungover. There's so much more to life."

Lee J., Manhattan College senior

"I know that my friends on many occasions say they have to stop drinking. This is usually Sunday afternoon after drinking for three days. So they don't drink until Thursday again. When Thursday comes around they think they have done something good. They reward themselves by going out and drinking. I think this is ridiculous because three out of seven days they spend lying around the house wanting to do nothing except watch television and sleep."

Anonymous

Success

COLLEGES AND UNIVERSITIES ACROSS THE COUNTRY are implementing a variety of alcohol and other drug education and abuse prevention programs. Some have been extremely beneficial, while others have met with limited success. Regardless of what your institution is doing, you can make the kinds of decisions that will minimize or eradicate the impact of high risk alcohol consumption in your life.

What I've tried to do in this book is educate you about the effects alcohol can have on your college career. You now know what alcohol is, how much alcohol is in a drink, how alcohol has affected many students' lives or the lives of their families, what the parties are sometimes like and so on. But what about you? How will you use this information? Hopefully you now realize that the decision to drink alcohol or not while in college is a serious one. When facing this decision, consider the following:

- What are your priorities in life?
- What are your family, religious and personal values?
- Do you have a history of alcoholism in your family?
- What is the school policy regarding alcohol consumption?
- Are you of legal drinking age? If not, do you understand the consequences you face if you are caught drinking?

If you have chosen to drink, continually monitor your consumption:
- How are your grades doing? Is your alcohol consumption affecting your academic performance?
- Is your tolerance increasing?
- Is your consumption affecting your relationships?
- For a complete assessment, review the "Identifying Problems" questionnaire in the "Addiction" chapter of this book.

Let me once again recommend the "Prime for Life" program, one of the most effective and informative alcohol-education programs available to college students. Developed by the Prevention Research Institute in Lexington, Kentucky, "Prime for Life" has been enthusiastically received by many college students across the country. If this course is not available on your campus, speak to your administrators. Let them know you are concerned about the presence of alcohol problems on your campus. Let them know you would like to have this program made available to all students, faculty and staff.

Peer Pressure

> *"One of the guys came over and asked me why I wasn't drinking. I told him I didn't feel like it. His response was, 'That's cool.' and walked away."*
>
> Jesse C., Georgia State University junior

In chapter one, "Party Time," students reported their experiences while attending a campus party and not drinking. Below are some of the specific comments by students regarding peer pressure, both positive and negative. As you will see, much of the pressures felt by students encourage high risk consumption. But we are also seeing a subtle shift of support toward abstinence as well. While reading these observations, consider how you would respond if you were in a similar situation. Also, consider how you react to someone at a party who is not drinking.

> "I also think that people respect me more when I go out to parties and don't drink at all. I think you are a pretty weak person if you give in to peer pressure."

> "When we got back to our room, we discussed the party a bit further. We all agreed that it was a little ridiculous how much people pressured us to drink. But, it also made us feel good to be able to stand our ground and say no."

> "When I found someone else who wasn't drinking I felt a lot more comfortable around her."

> "There was one real weird comment. This guy said I didn't look stoned. He assumed that if I wasn't drinking then I must have been smoking."

"People in general are more supportive if you choose not to drink."

"The peer pressure was unbelievable. People are used to me drinking so when they saw me without a cup they tried to drag me to the keg. When I responded no they just kept hounding me. I eventually grabbed a cup and held onto it so people thought I was drinking."

"I told people I wasn't drinking because I was too loaded the night before. It was a lie. It made me realize I was not secure enough in myself to tell people the main reason I didn't want to drink was because I didn't feel like it. I guess I felt I needed a better excuse than I just didn't feel like it."

"I never felt like there was any pressure to drink. That's high school stuff. I think people in college respect people's decisions about alcohol."

"The pressure to drink was not there like in high school. There is such a difference in the maturity levels between high school and college."

"I was not in the mood to have a beer and they understood and did not pressure me to drink. They respected me for my choice. I had a really great time and didn't have a drop of alcohol. Sometimes people do not know when to quit drinking and make real fools of themselves."

"I was constantly questioned as to why I was not drinking on that night. It was as if I was supposed to drink. However it was not just my friends asking me. I received constant encouragement from almost everyone around me to drink. It was like harassment. Somehow I had thought that it would be acceptable for me not to drink but the opposite was true."

"In our fraternity nobody is ever really criticized for not drinking. It's been a month since I did the project. I have had a few drinks at parties but I haven't gotten drunk. I drink to avoid the stupid questions about not drinking which can make you feel uncomfortable. Since I made this change I've been consuming fewer calories, saving money, no hangovers and my grades have improved."

"I noticed a lot of my friends trying to get me to drink. When I think of it, when I'm drinking I do the same thing. It's almost like you think something is wrong that the person isn't drinking. You think you are doing them a favor by filling their cup. It became annoying. I almost felt compelled to give some phony excuse. Not drinking because I didn't feel like it just wasn't enough."

"The pressure to drink lasted all night. I could not go up to someone and say a simple 'Hello.' I would always hear, 'Where the hell is your beer?', 'Aren't you drinking?', 'What's wrong with you?' I find it amusing to think that I was considered the one with the problem. Others were unaware that I was not drinking because they were too drunk to notice."

Do any of these remarks sound familiar? Remember, the choice to consume alcohol or not is *yours!* Often though, it is difficult for students to stick to a decision to abstain or consume in a low risk fashion. Below are some strategies for dealing with peer pressure.

Party Strategies

> *"At least now I know that if I don't feel like drinking I shouldn't go to one of these parties because all they end up being is annoying."*
>
> Melissa D., University of Vermont sophomore

> *"Sadly enough, I do not think someone can have as good of a time at a party without drinking."*
>
> Melanie M., University of Miami first-year student

> *"Not once in my three years at school have I seen soda or food served at fraternity parties. I live off-campus and whenever I have 'gatherings' of my own I always have snacks and non-alcoholic drinks."*
>
> Vincent A., Keene State College junior

> *"Sure, all we did was play board games and eat ice cream and snacks. But, it was fun. One of the good things was that we all remembered who we were with the night before plus we weren't hungover."*
>
> Bill M., University of Connecticut junior

"That is why we always have two designated sober people when we go out. They are responsible for driving and making sure we stay together. I wish we had started this practice two years ago before my friend was at a party, passed out and was raped."

Anonymous

Socialization is an important and exciting part of campus life. Parties can provide one way to meet new people. I *encourage* students to attend parties. But, once you have decided to attend a party, you're then faced with a number of other decisions. If you choose to drink alcohol, then you need to decide:

- What will you drink?
- How much will you drink?
- How fast will you drink?
- Will you eat?
- If you are underage, what are the consequences if you get caught?
- Will you participate in drinking games?
- Once you have reached your limit, how will you refuse offers to drink more?
- If you get impaired, how will you protect yourself?
- How will you get home?
- What about "hooking up"? Why should you? Who might it be? If you do, how will you feel about it in the morning?

To reduce your risk for impairment, try arriving at the party a little late and leaving a little early. Alternating an alcoholic drink with a non-alcoholic drink will also reduce your alcohol intake. Remember, you will probably get more impaired more quickly if you:

- are tired or getting over a recent illness
- have been taking medication
- have not eaten much during the day
- are premenstrual
- are feeling depressed

If you choose not to drink alcohol, then you need to decide:
- What will you drink?
- What will you do with your hands?
- How will you refuse offers to drink alcohol?

- What will you do later when many people may be drunk?

Activities

> *"I think everyone can use a break from parties and spend quality time with friends."*
>
> Monica A., Pennsylvania State University junior

> *"T.S. Eliot was obsessed with the idea of death within life; doing the same things over and over again and never experiencing new things. I am not the type of person who needs to drink four nights out of the week. I often try to find other things to do. But, there are a lot of other people who don't try to look beyond the party scene. I must say I feel sorry for someone who goes out looking for campus parties all the time and never seeks any new adventures."*
>
> Anonymous

> *"Why can't we think of things to do without alcohol or other drugs? It simply seems like when someone mentions the weekend, it means to stop being sober."*
>
> Anonymous

> *"I hope students don't go through what I did. I just wish they'd realize there are more ways to solve a problem or have fun than drinking and doing drugs."*
>
> Anonymous

> *"At the video store we saw many other students. It was good to know that not everyone was out getting hammered."*
>
> John S., Plymouth State College junior

When discussing the reasons why many students drink in excess, one of the most popular refrains is "There's nuthin' else to do!" I try to get my students to modify this statement by saying "There seems to be very little else to do that gives us the immediate satisfaction, relief and pleasure that drinking alcohol does, especially if I'm with a hundred or so others who are doing the same thing." Yes, it may seem that on your campus there aren't many diversions available that can give you the immediate satisfaction alcohol provides. But understand that there are many serious risks associated with this choice.

Is there really nuthin' else to do? Of course not! There are numerous things to do other than drink. Once my students admit that drinking is an easy and relatively cheap high, I have them sit down and list from A to Z some of the other ways they enjoy themselves and meet new people. Here are just some of the places and activities suggested:

Aerobics, Art, Acting, Assisting a Youth Group, Big Brother/Sister, Baseball, Basketball, Bicycling, Beach, Bungee Jumping, Board Games, Camping, Church, Crochet, Canoeing, Community cleanups, Coaching Little League, Cooking, Diving, Dancing, Driving the elderly to shopping, Easter Baskets for needy children, Feeding the hungry in a soup kitchen, Frisbee Golf, Flying, Figure Skating, Fooseball, Fishing, Golf, Gardening, Hang Gliding, Horseback riding, Hiking, Helping the Homeless, Hockey, Ice Climbing, Internships, Jogging, Juggling, Kite Flying, Knitting, Learning a new skill, Library, Laundromat, Meditation, Movies, Museums, Malls, Nintendo, Needlepoint, Newspaper Staff, Opera, Prayer, Painting, Playing Music, Politics, Pool, Ping Pong, Quarry Diving, Rock Climbing, Reading, Rafting, Running, Roller Blading, Shopping, Studying, Surfing, Skiing, Snow Boarding, Sculpting, Student Government, Sailing, Scavenger Hunts, Sewing, Triathlons, Talking with friends, Tennis, Tubing, Theater, Ultimate Frisbee, Visiting the elderly, Video Games, Volunteering, Walking, Weight Lifting, Whale Watching, Work Study, Writing, Wind Surfing, Wrestling, Xerox Art, Xylophone Practice, Yoga, Yearbook Staff, Yard Sales, Zoos (OK - the Xs are a stretch!)

These are just some of the ways to enjoy yourself or perhaps meet and socialize with your peers and the neighboring community. So there are plenty of alternatives to drinking. They may not provide the same immediate satisfaction, but I guarantee you'll feel better in the morning after participating in some of these activities. A few students have commented to me that many of the activities on the list take place during the day and are not alternatives to drinking. True, but for many of these activities a good night's sleep is essential for optimal performance. If I am going rock climbing or skiing, I want a clear head in the morning. If I am going to be interacting with children, the elderly or a homeless person, a hangover will certainly rob me of the essence of that interaction.

Often students claim the reason they do not participate in some of the activities listed above is a lack of money. But consider this: It is estimated that in one year,

U.S. college students will spend $5.5 billion on alcohol—more than they spend on soft drinks, tea, milk, coffee and books combined. On a typical campus, annual per capita student spending for alcohol—$446 per student—far exceeds the per-capita budget of the college library.[84] Don't fall into the "There's nuthin' else to do" trap. Get out and enjoy life. Sure—go to the parties. Meet new people and make new friends. But take advantage of the world beyond the campus walls! And do it with your new friends from the college and the community.

GET REAL

College can provide you with wonderful opportunities to expand your horizons as a human being. You are the only person, however, who can make this happen. And, it can happen if you *GET REAL:*

Goals: Developing specific long-term and short-term goals will give you focus and direction. Consider what would you like to be doing in ten years. Five years. During the next year. Consider what you need to do to accomplish your long range goals. When faced with important day-to-day decisions, ask yourself how your alternatives fit into the attainment of your goals. By listing and committing to your goals, choices about alcohol consumption will be much easier to make.

Education: Your primary reason for being in college is to become better educated—don't lose sight of that. Academics are your number-one priority. When making decisions about courses, examine how they fit into your goals. And, a large portion of your education will take place beyond the classroom walls and the library stacks. Be sure you place yourself in an environment where your experiences will contribute to the accomplishment of your goals.

Tradition: Most colleges have a rich history of tradition and school spirit. Become a part of it. Intercollegiate athletics provide one way to get involved with your school. However, if your school specializes in research, learn about its important contributions to science. Learn about famous graduates. Also, attend cultural events including plays, concerts, debates and other presentations. It may sound trite, but developing a sense of school spirit and knowing the fine traditions of your school will help you feel more connected not only to your school but also your peers.

Responsibility: It is time for you to take responsibility for your own life. You can no longer blame your parents, your teachers, your friends or anyone else for your difficulties. Take charge of your life and pursue your goals.

Enthusiasm: Whatever you choose to do in college, do it enthusiastically. Study hard, work hard and play hard. College will mean more to you if you make a commitment to all your endeavors. Associate with successful students, faculty and staff. Remember success breeds success.

Activities: Seek out new, exciting and enriching activities and people. Don't get caught in a rut filled with the same old parties and the same old drinking. There's plenty to do on campus and in the surrounding community. Reaching out to others through community service-oriented activities will provide you with memories and inspiration that will last a lifetime.

Love: Your life will be more profoundly satisfying and your interactions with others will be much more meaningful if you follow the fundamental guiding principle of "Love your neighbor as yourself." And, opening your heart to God or your understanding of a Higher Power will comfort you during some of the difficult times you may experience while in college. Your choice to pursue a spiritual path, and the love that pursuit can generate, are the most important aspects of human existence. If your family has a religious heritage which has been lost, talk to your parents, grandparents, great grandparents or family friends about the impact of its loss. If you practiced a particular religion prior to college, don't abandon it—celebrate it!

Get real! Achieving success in your life starts now. It starts with a clear understanding of what it means to be successful. I believe Ralph Waldo Emerson captured the essence of success in the following:

Success
*To laugh often; to win the respect of intelligent
people and the affection of children; to earn the
appreciation of honest critics and endure the
betrayal of false friends; to appreciate beauty, to
find the best in others; to leave the world a bit
better, whether by a healthy child, a garden
patch or a redeemed social condition; to know
even one life has breathed a little easier because
you have lived. This is to have succeeded.*

Personal Challenge: Campus Activities

Goal:

To increase participation in a variety of co-curricular activities.

Instructions:

1. List several recreational activities which you presently enjoy and identify which of these activities is available both on the campus and in the local community.

2. List several recreational activities you believe you might enjoy and identify which of these activities is available both on the campus and in the local community.

3. Create an action plan for exploring each recreational activity which interests you by researching the following information:
>   a. Cost
>   b. Distance from campus
>   c. Directions
>   d. Others who might enjoy the activity

Reflections:

a. Are recreational activities important to you? What need might these activities play in your college career?
b. Were you aware of how many recreational options were available to you on this campus and in this community? Are you likely to take advantage of these activities? Why? Why not?
c. Have you found new activities that are available that you would like to try? What would encourage you to test out a new recreational activity?
d. Does alcohol consumption impact your ability to participate in your recreational activities?

Adapted from Activities Manual for The Education of Character, Lessons for Beginners, Will Keim (1995). Harcourt Brace College Publishers

Epilogue

WHEN I DISCUSS ALCOHOL and other drug use with my students and students across the country, I acknowledge my own excessive alcohol and other drug use while in college. I discuss the pleasures and the problems I experienced as a result of those excessive indulgences. More often than not, a student will say "Jim, that's not fair! You had your fun and now you're trying to ruin ours!"

First of all, get used to it. Life is not fair. When I was in college, society was somehow unaware of, or actually denied, the true toll that alcohol-related car crashes were having on our generation. When I was in college, sex was not a death-defying feat. We considered safe sex as having a girlfriend who was on the pill. When I was in college most of us considered pot harmless. Is it fair that we now have stricter DUI laws? Is it fair that you need to consider the possibility of AIDS every time you have a sexual encounter? Is it fair that we now know that marijuana is even more harmful than we ever suspected in the sixties? No, it's not fair. But, life is not fair.

Yes I did have some great times in college. But I have also paid a very dear price for it. There has been a great deal of pain and difficulty in my life that is not noticeable now. Yes, I learned a great deal about myself through this pain, but I wish I had gained this self-awareness through more constructive means. I'm not sure whether or not I will ever really reach my true potential as a person—and I'll never know. There were so many lost years.

No one is trying to ruin your fun. My goal and the goal of most campus prevention specialists is to enlighten you as to the many serious risks associated with alcohol and other drug use. With this enlightenment we also want to provide you with the alternatives and skills needed to help you avoid the problems associated with alcohol and other drug use.

This book began with some words of wisdom from a student. It seems appropriate to end with them also:

"Don't let the time of your life ruin the rest of your life."

Group Challenges

Group Challenge: Advertising

Goal:

To heighten awareness of advertising themes and techniques.

Instructions:

1. Separate class into small groups. Each group should select a leader and a recorder for the group. This leader will make certain the group process moves along smoothly throughout the exercise. If there is more than one group, the recorder will summarize the content (information) and process (method by which the content was obtained) of their group activity.

2. Overnight Assignment - Each member of the group selects five alcohol commercials from television and/or newspaper or magazines ads to review.

3. At the next group meeting, each member reports back to the small group with copies of videotapes and/or ads and provides the following information:

     a. How was the use of alcohol portrayed in the ad?

     b. How were the drinkers portrayed in the ad?

     c. What do you think is the theme of the ad? (i.e. sexual innuendo, adventure, fun, romance, etc.)

4. Small groups generate a list of the themes of the alcohol commercials and/or ads.

5. Small groups report back to the class the themes they identified regarding how alcohol was portrayed in their commercials and/or ads.

6. Class discusses the results of this exercise.

Personal Reflections:

a. Based on your own experiences, how accurate is the portrayal of alcohol consumption in the media?

b. How do you think young adults are influenced by commercials and ads?

c. How have your attitudes about alcohol been influenced by commercials and ads?

d. Have your attitudes about alcohol advertising changed as a result of this exercise?

Group Challenge: Campus Advertising

Goal:

To provide students an opportunity to identify and discuss freely their beliefs regarding campus alcohol advertising while identifying critical issues faced by campus administrators regarding this advertising.

Instructions:

1. Separate class into two groups. Each group should select a leader and a recorder for the group. This leader will make certain the group process moves along smoothly throughout the exercise. If there is more than one group, the recorder will summarize the content (information) and process (method by which the content was obtained) of their group activity.
2. One group is assigned the Pro position and the other group is assigned the Con position to an issue listed below.
3. Debate the issue.
4. For the next issue, each group is assigned the opposite position. (The Cons become the Pros and vice versa.)

Issues:

1. Sponsorship of college athletic events by the alcohol industry
2. Alcohol advertising during televised college athletic events
3. Spring Break advertisements by the alcohol industry
4. Alcohol advertising in campus newspapers and on campus radio stations
5. Anti-alcohol messages (newspapers, campus radio, posters, etc.) on the college campus

Personal Reflections:

a. How does your campus handle alcohol advertising? Do you believe your campus implements a responsible policy regarding campus alcohol advertising?
b. Is there anything you can do to address alcohol advertising on your campus?

Adapted from Making Choices: A Personal Look at Alcohol & Drug Use (1992). McGraw-Hill Higher Education, Quinn/Scaffa

Group Challenges

Group Challenge: Other Drugs

Goal:

To understand the physical, psychological and emotional consequences of the use of a variety of drugs.

Instructions:

1. Separate class into small groups. Each group should select a leader and a recorder for the group. This leader will make certain the group process moves along smoothly throughout the exercise. If there is more than one group, the recorder will summarize the content (information) and process (method by which the content was obtained) of their group activity.

2. Each group selects one drug to research. Cocaine, LSD, Marijuana, Ecstasy, Heroin

3. Overnight Assignment - Using five separate resources (other than this book) find the answers to the following questions:

      a. What are the dangers of being under the influence of this drug?

      b. Is this drug addictive?

      c. What are the physical and psychological implications of both short term and long term use?

4. Members of each small group report their findings to their own group.

5. Each small group synthesizes the findings of its members.

6. Small groups report their findings to the classs.

Personal Reflections:

a. How does this information influence your decision to use or not use these drugs?

b. Do you believe that you are not susceptible to the dangers reported about these drugs? Why or why not?

c. How could the use of these drugs impact your success in college and beyond?

Group Challenge: Stress

Goal:
To identify the major causes of stress in students' lives and develop an action plan for stress reduction.

Instructions:
1. Each student records on a piece of paper three major sources of stress in his/her life.
2. Synthesize all the responses into one large list on a flip chart or chalkboard.
3. Class determines how these sources of stress can be grouped together into more general issues. (A typical list might include time management, over commitment, interpersonal conflict, disorganization, test anxiety, family problems, other personal problem, etc.)
4. Class breaks into issue-based groups based on the applicability of it to each student. Each group should select a leader and a recorder for the group. This leader will make certain the group process moves along smoothly throughout the exercise. If there is more than one group, the recorder will summarize the content (information) and process (method by which the content was obtained) of their group activity.
5. Each group discusses ways to reduce the stress caused by the issue selected by the group. Each student should be encouraged to speak out on the issue. The recorder notes the action plan(s) developed by the group. The action plan should be as specific as possible.
6. Reconvene as a class. Each recorder reports the action plan(s) for reducing stress surrounding their issue.

Personal Reflections:

a. Where does your stress come from? Faulty interpersonal skills? Faulty organizational skills?
b. Can skill development help you reduce or manage your stress more effectively?
c. What one new skill or behavior would reduce your stress substantially?
d. Which action plan(s) is appropriate for you?
e. Are there ways other students can help you reduce your stress rather than your trying to solve it alone?
f. Does high risk alcohol consumption and the resulting consequences contribute to your stress?

Adapted from Activities Manual for The Education of Character, Lessons for Beginners, Will Keim (1995). Harcourt Brace College Publishers

Group Challenges

Group Challenge: Activities

Goal:
To broaden student perspective on activities that can be done on a date or with other friends.

Instructions:
1. Each student records a list of ten things that would each cost $20.00 or less that s/he could do on a date.
2. Separate class into small groups and share your lists. Each group should select a leader and a recorder for the group. This leader will make certain the group process moves along smoothly throughout the exercise. If there is more than one group, the recorder will summarize the content (information) and process (method by which the content was obtained) of their group activity.
3. Small groups create one large list containing all of the ideas from each member of the group.
4. Small groups brainstorm as many more activities as possible in five minutes.
5. Small groups report their lists back to the class.

Personal Reflections:
a. Think about recent times that have been enjoyable or fun for you. What were you doing? Were you spending a lot of money? If yes, could you have had as much fun without spending as much money? Are there other ways for you to have fun without spending a lot of money?
b. How important is spending money when having fun with a friend or date?
c. How does high risk alcohol consumption impact the cost of having fun or dating?

Adapted from Activities Manual for The Education of Character, Lessons for

Beginners, Will Keim (1995). Harcourt Brace College PublishersReflections:

Group Challenge: Parties

Goal:

To understand the different perspectives that men and women have regarding party behaviors.

Instructions:

1. Separate class into small groups. Each group should select a leader and a recorder for the group. This leader will make certain the group process moves along smoothly throughout the exercise. If there is more than one group, the recorder will summarize the content (information) and process (method by which the content was obtained) of their group activity.

2. The class leader reads a descriptive statement from the chapter one "Party Time" comments of the students who attended the party and did not consume alcohol.

3. Following each statement, members of each group vote as to whether it was a "male" or "female" making the statement.

4. Members of the small groups discuss why they picked "male" or "female" following each statement.

5. Following discussion and voting for each statement, small groups will report back to the class the reults of their voting.

Personal Reflections:

a. What surprised you about the perspectives that others have about men and women?

Group Challenge: Why College?

Goal:

In a group setting, to create a hierarchical list of the primary reasons for attending college.

Instructions:

1. Seperate class into small groups. Each group should select a leader and a recorder for the group. This leader will make certain the group process moves along smoothly throughout the exercise. If there is more than one group, the recorder will summarize the content (information) and process (method by which the content was obtained) of their group activity.

2. Each member of the group writes down the primary reason why s/he is attending college. The reasons can be a mix of practical, i.e. "to get a job," and philosophical, i.e. "to gain wisdom."

3. After each student has written his/her reasons, through a consensus process, the leader rank-orders all the reason for attending college from the members. The group should decide which reason is most important and second most important, etc. Each group must arrive at this list through discussion and reasoning and without averaging, "horse trading" (you vote for my first choice and I'll vote for our choice), or "majority rule" voting.

4. Small groups report their lists back to the class.

Personal Reflections:

a. What are your goals for your college education?

b. Were you surprised by some of the members and their reasons for getting an education?

c. Have you gained some additional short-term and long-term goals from this activity?

Adapted from Activities Manual for The Education of Character, Lessons for Beginners, Will Keim (1995). Harcourt Brace College Publishers

Group Challenge: Attitudes about Sex

Goal:

To gain a deeper understanding of the attitudes and opinions of other students regarding sexual activity.

Instructions:

1. Place signs around the room indicating the following five responses.

Strongly Agree   *Agree*   *Not Sure*   *Disagree*   *Strongly Disagree*

2. Class leader reads one of the statements listed below.
3. After reading a statement, members of the group move to the sign in the room indicating their own response to the statement.
4. Members of each group explain their reasons for their answer.

Statements:

a. Sometimes men get so turned on with a woman, they just can't stop.

b. Sometimes women get so turned on with a man, they just can't stop.

c. If a man and woman have been touching and fooling around all evening, both of them must want to have intercourse.

d. A man can have sex with his date and does not need to get her agreement if they have had sex before.

e. A woman who goes to a man's room after a party clearly wants to have sex.

f. A man who goes to a woman's room after a party clearly wants to have sex.

g. If a man spends a lot of money on a date, he is entitled to sex.

h. Someone who is impaired due to alcohol use, cannot give informed consent for sexual activity.

i. Kissing, fondling, etc. is an indication that a person wants to engage in sexual intercourse.

j. Drinking causes people to engage in sexual activity they would not normally do.

Adapted from Alcohol and Acquaintance Rape: Strategies to Protect Yourself and

Group Challenges

Each Other. The Higher Education Center for Alcohol and Other Drug Prevention, US Department of Education, 1996.

Group Challenge: Attitudes about Alcohol

Goal:

To gain a deeper understanding of the attitudes and opinions of other students regarding the use of alcohol..

Instructions:

1. Place signs around the room indicating the following five responses.

Strongly Agree   *Agree*   *Not Sure*   *Disagree*   *Strongly Disagree*

2. Class leader reads one of the statements listed below.
3. After reading a statement, members of the class move to the sign in the room indicating their own response to the statement.
4. Members of each group explain their reasons for their answer.

Statements:

a. I can have a few drinks without my driving being affected.
b. Alcohol helps me get through stressful situations.
c. Drinking regularly could result in my becoming addicted to alcohol.
d. Drinking alcohol is bad for my health.
e. I have more fun at social events when I drink.
f. Alcohol has been a negative influence on my life.
g. My friendships would be damaged if I drank a lot.
h. I feel more confident when I drink alcohol.
i. Drinking alcohol is a good way for me to relax and loosen up.
j. I would feel ashamed if I drank too much.
k. I would have problems at school if I drank more than I do now.
l. Drinking is a good way to forget my problems.
m. It is okay if I get drunk once in awhile.
n. Drinking alcohol is a normal part of the college experience.

Group Challenge: Dating

Goal:

To develop a heightened awareness of "likes" and "dislikes" of dating behavior.

Instructions:

1. Divide the class with women on one side of the room and men on the other side.
2. Each group will develop two lists:
   - The first list will include all of the groups answers to the following:
       "I really like it when my dating partner..."

   - The second list will include all of the groups answers to the following:
       "I really hate it when my dating partner..."

3. Each group will report their lists back to the other group, taking turns with statements from each list.

4. As a class discuss the following:
a. Do you need any statements clarified?
b. How were your lists similar?
c. How were your lists different?
d. Can you make any generalizations about what you as a class really like and really dislike about the dating experience?

Personal Reflections:

a. How can alcohol impact your behavior while on a date?
b. Have you done any of the things on either list when on a date? How did your date react when you did?

Adapted from Activities Manual for The Education of Character, Lessons for Beginners, Will Keim (1995). Harcourt Brace College Publishers

Challenge Results

Chapter 2 Alcohol: Estimating BAL

Exercise 1:
10 Drinks (Male) - 200 Pound = .20 - .04 (.01 x 4 hours = .04) =
.16 BAL after 4 Hours and 10 Drinks
Giving coffee to someone who has been drinking will not sober up the drinker. All it will do is wake up the drinker. This could be dangerous because it could possibly cause the drinker to feel that s/he is okay to drive since they are more awake. However, the coffee does nothing to reduce the impairment level of the drinker!

Exercise 2:
14 Drinks (Female) - 125 Pound Female = .59 - .02 (.01 x 2 hours = .02) =
.57 BAL after 2 Hours and 14 Drinks
She is probably dead. By the way, just like the coffee, a cold shower will simply wake up the drinker not sober her/him up. It could also cause the drinker to suffer a heart attack.

Exercise 3:
6 Drinks (Male) - 180 Pound Male = .15 - .04 (.01 x 4 hours = .04) =
.11 BAL after 4 Hours and 6 Drinks
6 Drinks (Male) - 200 Pound Male = .13 - .04 (.01 x 4 hours = .04) =
.09 BAL after 4 Hours and 6 Drinks
In order to correctly answer the question regarding the DUI ticket, you must know your own state's current regulations. What is the minimum BAL at a given age that will result in a DUI ticket in your state? What are the consequences for someone underage caught drinking and driving at any BAL?

Exercise 4:
.18 - .08 (.01 x 8 hours) = **.10 BAL after 8 Hours**
If you drove to the campus, you could have gotten a DUI ticket from the police. Sleep simply provides rest for the drinker. It does not "sober up" a person.

Chapter 3 Drinks: Attitudes About Acohol

#	STRONGLY AGREE	AGREE	NOT SURE	DISAGREE	STRONLY DISAGREE
1.	1	2	3	4	5
2.	1	2	3	4	5
3.	1	2	3	4	5
4.	5	4	3	2	1
5.	5	4	3	2	1
6.	5	4	3	2	1
7.	5	4	3	2	1
8.	1	2	3	4	5
9.	5	4	3	2	1
10.	5	4	3	2	1
11.	1	2	3	4	5
12.	1	2	3	4	5
13.	5	4	3	2	1
14.	5	4	3	2	1
15.	5	4	3	2	1
16.	1	2	3	4	5
17.	1	2	3	4	5
18.	5	4	3	2	1
19.	1	2	3	4	5
20.	1	2	3	4	5

- Circle your score for each question.
- Add the point values.
- Divide the total by 20.

Evaluation:

- The maximum score of five (5) indicates you believe using alcohol can be DETRIMENTAL to your social, emotional and physical well being.

- The minimum score of one (1) indicates you believe using alcohol can ENHANCE your social, emotional and physical well being.

Personal Reflections:

Challenge Results

How much do you rely on alcohol to enhance your life?

Chapter 6 Addiction:
Identifying Alcohol Problems
Evaluation:
A YES answer to one question is a warning.
A YES answer to as few as three questions indicates that alcohol has become or is becoming a problem.

Chapter 8 Family Issues: Family Health

For each correct answer, give yourself one point:

1. true	4. false	7. true	10. false
2. true	5. false	8. true	11. false
3. true	6. false	9. true	12. false

Evaluation:
10-12 points = you are lucky to be part of a healthy and functional family.
4-9 points = you have a family that tends to be functional but has some characteristics
1-3 points = you have a family that is dysfunctional and unhealthy. Alcoholism, drug abuse, physical/sexual abuse may also be present. Professional help is seriously recommended.

Chapter 12 Advertising: Drinking Choices

Score your responses to each statement.
Definitely Yes = 5
Probably Yes = 4
Maybe = 3
Probably No = 2
Definitely No = 1
- Add the point values.
- Divide the total by 20.

Evaluation:
The maximum score of five (5) indicates you are STRONGLY INFLUENCED to drink in a wide variety of situations. A score in the mid-range indicates that under some circumstances you MAY BE INFLUENCED to drink. A lower score around one (1) indicates you are RARELY INFLUENCED to drink regardless of the situation.

Resources

Resources

The following is a list of websites that may be of interest or value to you. This is by no means a comprehensive list. New sites appear almost everyday and some of these may disappear by the time you get this book. Appearance on this list does not indicate complete endorsement of all the contents of all the sites. When using a website as a source for information regarding alcohol or other drugs, be very careful about who or what organization is sponsoring the site. Some sites may contain inaccurate or biased information.

Alcohol and Drug Abuse Prevention Team (ADAPT):
http://showme.missouri.edu
Focuses on providing awareness of alcohol related issues and promotes abstinence and/or low risk drinking. It also promotes the PARTY (Promoting Alcohol Responsibility Through You) program. Also available are statistics on patterns of use as well as links to other related sites for college students.

Alcohol and Your College Experience:
http://www.factsontap.org
Presents information on many aspects of alcohol and college students including tips for how to cut down on your drinking and a test to see if you drink too much. It includes information on alcohol including how it relates to: sexual experiences, effects on the body, determining your blood alcohol level and much more. There are updates on news events that are related to alcohol and college life as well.

BRAD 21 Program:
http://www.brad21.org
Sponsored by the family and friends of Bradley McCue, a Michigan State student who died of alcohol poisoning on his twenty-first birthday. The purpose of this site is to educate young adults about the low risk use of alcohol and the effects that alcohol can have on others. Information describes: the effects of alcohol on the body, how to recognize the effects on yourself and others, how to encourage abstinence or low risk use, and how to determine when medical assistance is needed.

College Parents of America (CPA):
http://collegeparents.org
Designed to help parents prepare for their child's college life including information ranging from getting financial help for tuition to finding links to different resources on combating high risk alcohol use by their child. There is excellent information for parents regarding talking to their son/daughter about binge drinking, responsible behavior, safe spring breaks and much more.

George Washington University Substance Abuse Prevention Center:
http://www.gu.edu/~sapc/
Presents information on sexual assault, stress management, alcohol and drug policies plus tips on how to have a safe party experience Also found here are facts on the rate of first

time drug users. The goal for this site is to increase abstinence and/or low risk drinking and awareness of possible consequences.

Go Ask Alice:
http://www.goaskalice.columbia.edu

Post any health related question on any topic. Areas of interest include but are not limited to: relationships, sexual health, alcohol/drug issues, emotional health, and fitness. View any question and answer that had been asked previously about the topic in which you are interested. All postings and inquiries are anonymous.

Had Enough:
http://www.hadenough.org

Focuses on students who have had enough with binge drinking and the effects that it has on campus life. It gives support for students who are trying to decrease binge drinking on college campuses. There is ample information about binge drinking and the effects it has on the drinker and those surrounding the drinker.

Harvard School of Public Health:
http://www.hsph.harvard.edu/cas/

Provides statistics and research articles based on the Harvard School of Public Health College Alcohol Study, an ongoing survey of over 15,000 students at 140 four year colleges in 40 states. The CAS study examines high risk behaviors among college students such as episodic or binge drinking, smoking, illicit drug use, gun possession, violence, and other behavioral, social and health problems confronting today's college students.

Inter-Association Task Force on Alcohol and Other Substance Abuse Issues:
http://www.iatf.org

Provides tips to campus officials on how to implement a task force for leadership on health issues, residential life, student life, student government and many others. Also available is information on how to train campus leaders about alcohol and other drug issues.

Promising Practices - Campus Alcohol Strategies:
http://www.promprac.gmu.edu

Presents education on elimination of alcohol and other drug abuse on college campuses. There is information on the consequences of use and how to help your campus. This site encourages students to think about their lifestyle and how to make healthy decisions. There is an online forum as well to discuss your concerns.

Student Affairs:
http://www.siu.edu/staffair/

Promotes the enhancement of student development through services and education. This site encourages students to get involved in different organizations and to be successful academically.

The Core Institute:
http://www.siu.edu/~coreinst

Developed by Southern Illinois University at Carbondale, this site assists colleges in drug and alcohol prevention efforts by providing the latest statistics on campus drug/alcohol use and violence based on the Core Survey which is administered on campuses nationwide. Copies of surveys for students, faculty and staff are available. Online advice and help are offered as well.

The Higher Education Center for Alcohol and Other Drug Prevention:
http://www.edc.org/hec
Offers strategies to change culture on campuses and prevent illegal alcohol and other drug use. Supported by the U.S. Department of Education, the Higher Education Center supports all institutions in their efforts to address alcohol and other drug problems. Information on how to participate in training workshops conducted by the Higher Education Center is available from this site.

Training for Intervention Procedures (TIPS):
http://www.gettips.com
Contains information about the TIPS program. TIPS conducts workshops for bartenders and waiters to develop the skills and confidence necessary to prevent customer intoxication. Information on the prevention of impaired driving and underage drinking is provided as well. Upcoming workshops are also posted.

Will Keim Speaks:
http://www.will keim.com
Contains information on the outstanding speaker Will Keim. He has lectured to over two million students on a variety of topics from Greek life to communication skills. His schedule and copies of some presentations are posted here.

Alcohol and Other Drug Information

Alcohol Information and Education:
http://www.lcb.state.pa.us/edu/start
Offers tips on how to make wise choices, how to start local campaigns, how to prevent underage drinking and examples of how someone with an alcohol problem may act. Statistics on accidents and other issues related to alcohol use are also offered. There is an impairment chart that helps people realize their estimated intoxication level depending on their sex, weight, height and number of drinks consumed.

American Council for Drug Education:
http://www.acde.org
Discusses the effects that different substances have on the body and their impact on relationships with others. This site contains tips for parents on how to talk to their children about substance use and how to notice if their child is using an illegal substance. This council is part of the Phoenix House program and offers information on substance abuse education and prevention.

American Medical Association Office of Alcohol and Other Drug Abuse:
http://ww.ama-assn.org/special/aos/index.htm
Lists policies on alcohol use, information on Alanon and Alateen, as well as facts on college life and consumption of alcohol. The site also provides information on the A.M.A. "A Matter of Degree" program for college students.

Center for Science in the Public Interest (CSPI):
http://www.cspinet.org
Offers a wide range of information including nutrition, jobs and alcohol. The site addresses issues related to alcohol use including advertisements and promotions. There are many links to other sites of interest and information on a special alcohol policy project that helps to reduce use. This site provides statistics proving that alcohol is the leading cause of premature deaths in the United States.

Center for Substance Abuse Prevention (CSAP):
http://www.covesoft.com/csap.html
Provides assistance to community projects concerning alcohol and other drugs. The goal of these projects is to give information that will build skills and competence rather than dependence. CSAP offers trainers for community support and assistance with project development.

Dr. Drew:
http://www.drdrew.com
Based around the popular MTV show "Loveline," this site offers information on a variety of issues from general health to sex and alcohol. There is an opportunity to ask Dr. Drew a question with his response found on the online forum. If you need to get help with any issue in particular, this site offers several resources for you.

Healthfinder:
http://www.healthfinder.gov
Provides information on diseases, nutrition, STDs, alcohol use and other issues. This site is a database for most health-related topics. There are links specialized for different age groups, gender and special populations all related to health issues.

Jean Kilbourne:
http://www.jeankilbourne.com
Provides information on the pioneering work that Jean Kilbourne has done on alcohol and tobacco advertisements and the image of women in these advertisements. She has written a number of books and is an acclaimed lecturer on these issues. There is a list of resources for various topics she covers in her work as well as her schedule, her availability and her contact information.

Join Together Online:
http://www.jointogether.org
Addresses efforts to reduce gun violence and substance abuse. There are news articles on each of these efforts as well as a photo gallery that shows real life consequences of violence.

Resources

There is a quick search database for substance abuse and violence issues. The site also contains information regarding the "Demand Treatment" program which initiates the demand for treatment for addicts.

Marin Institute for the Prevention of Alcohol & Other Drug Problems:
http://www.marininstitute.org
Provides information to assist in confronting those who profit from alcohol sales and create harmful conditions to others. There is a schedule and registration information for training sessions provided by the organization on how to deal with these issues. Links to alcohol beverage sites, information on their advertisements and research findings can be viewed as well.

Marin Institute on Prevention of Alcohol & Other Drug Problems: alcohol policy and industry database:
http://www.andornot.com/marin
Provides a database from the Marin Institute for research on the alcohol beverage industry, policies and prevention efforts. There is information from 1991-present available from a variety of sources.

Monitoring the Future (MTF):
http://www.monitoringthefuture.org/
Focuses on drug use and abuse with information on recent trends in use of alcohol and other drugs, links to related sites as well as data bases and copies of available press releases related to alcohol and drug use. It contains information on studies performed on the behaviors, attitudes and values of secondary and college students as well as other young adults in America.

Mothers Against Drunk Driving (MADD):
http://www.madd.org
Supports those who have lost a loved one due to an alcohol related car crash. This is a nonprofit organization supported by mothers who are looking for solutions to impaired driving and underage drinking. Other information provided includes statistics for any zip code you wish to research, how to become a member, different programs offered and much more.

National Center on Addiction & Substance Abuse (CASA/ Columbia University):
http://www.casacolumbia.org
Provides research results on public opinion, program demonstrations, policy development and medical studies. CASA examines the social cost of alcohol and how it affects everyone around the user. There is an assessment of what helps and what doesn't during an intervention and also gives suggestions for those who are looking to get help for their problem.

National Clearinghouse for Alcohol and Drug Information:
http://www.health.org
Provides an information database as well as a quick fact page and an online forum. Through work with the Center for Substance Abuse and the U.S. Department of Health and Human Services, this site provides information on substance use.

National Council on Alcohol and Drug Dependence:
http://www.ncadd.org
Attempts to eradicate the stigma of the disease of alcoholism and educates Americans on the disease nature of addiction. The site indicates how addiction is a disease that is not only avoidable but also treatable. It provides information on health and medical issues as well as information for both parents and students who need help to talk to each other about substance use. An online message board allows visitors of the site to ask Dr. Bob a question and receive an answer on the web page.

National Institute on Alcohol Abuse and Alcoholism:
http://www.niaaa.nih.gov
Provides information on NIAAA research on the causes, consequences, treatment, and prevention of alcoholism and other alcohol-related problems. NIAAA is part of the National Institute of Health and provides information on all topics of alcohol use and abuse. Links to other sites and databases are provided in addition to the research information.

Partnership for a Drug Free America:
http://www.drugfreeamerica.org
Aims to reduce the demand for illicit drugs in America through media communication. The site links to sites on prevention, treatment, mentoring, counseling, health, and teens.

PREVLINE: Prevention Online:
http://www.health.org
Contains links to a variety of resources on drug use and abuse, as well as current statistics on the level of use in the United States. Information relevant to specific age groups and ethnic backgrounds is also available. Many resources can be located through this site.

Robert Wood Johnson Foundation:
http://www.rwjf.org/main.html
Provides information regarding grants funded through the Robert Wood Johnson Foundation. These grants fund research for many areas including: tobacco, alcohol, illicit drugs and mulit-use drugs. Information on treatment, prevention and enforcement are among the subjects that are detailed.

Educational Materials

Beer, Booze and Behavior:
http://www.lasalle.edu/~chapman/assess.htm
Informs students and others about opportunities for socialization and recreation other than drinking or other drug use. There are ideas for other things to do as well as how to confront people who drink and abuse the rights and properties of other people. Many links to sites of interest related to alcohol use and other issues are available. A virtual reality scenario allows you to plug in your personal statistics, then go through a drinking episode to estimate your blood alcohol level as you drink.

Resources

Center for Education and Drug Abuse Research:
http://cedar.pharmacy.pitt.edu/main.html
Presents the results of research conducted by CEDAR regarding how families and other social groups interact with substance use and abuse.

FACE Truth and Clarity in Alcohol:
http://www.faceproject.org
Provides information regarding FACE, a national non-profit organization that focuses specifically on alcohol issues. FACE conducts work in three areas: media development, training and national advocacy. FACE aims to reduce the risks related to alcohol sales and increase the safety factors related to alcohol consumption. Information on their research topics and findings as well as low risk consumption guidelines are detailed here.

The Intoximeters Incorporated:
http://www.intox.com/Drink_Wheel.html
Provides a form to assist in estimating your blood/breath alcohol concentration based on the information provided. Its purpose is to provide information about the low risk use of alcohol.

Prevention Research Institute, Inc. (PRI):
http://www.askpri.org
Provides information about the programs conducted by PRI. The goal of PRI is to reduce the incidence of alcohol and drug-related problems in the United States and other countries through a lifestyle related risk reduction program. Programs designed by PRI are designed to persuade resistant audiences to examine and change their attitudes and behaviors concerning alcohol and drug use.

RU Aware? Alcohol Education Page:
http://www.runet.edu/~kcastleb/toc.html
Educates college students about alcohol, the facts surrounding alcohol and its consumption and how to deal with someone who is drunk. There is an alcohol awareness quiz as well as information on how alcohol affects you and myths pertaining to alcohol consumption among other topics.

Searching the Internet for Drug Information:
http://www.drugs.indiana.edu/pubs/newsline/searching.html
Discusses how some web pages are filled with useless information and how to detect if the information is correct. There are lists of different search engines that can be trusted to find accurate information on the Internet as well as a specific directory for information pertaining to alcohol and other drugs.

Greek Life

National Intrafraternity Conference:
http://www.nicindy.org
Provides a variety of services to support and enhance the fraternity movement throughout

the United States and Canada including: educational conferences; videotapes; workbooks and manuals; campus consultations.

National Panhellenic Conference
http://www.npcwomen.com
Provides information regarding NPC conferences, publications and services dedicated to the betterment of sorority life.

Peer Outreach Programs

BACCHUS/GAMMA Peer Education Networks:
http://www.bacchusgamma.org
Assists students and administrators in developing a peer outreach effort on their campus. There is information on different campus-related topics as well as tips for those who are in leadership positions. This site provides program ideas, research information and statistics, a chat room with different topics for each session and information about becoming a member. Information on developing a BACCHUS/GAMMA chapter on your campus is also available.

Advocates for Youth:
http://advocatesforyouth.org/peered.htm
Focuses on helping young people make wise choices with regard to sexual interactions. This group attempts to disprove the myths that people hear and believe about sex, and correctly inform them about the challenges that sexual relations hold and their possible consequences. There is an opportunity at this site to ask a peer educator questions on health or sex issues. A response is e-mailed to the inquirer as quickly as possible. Links to other peer educator resources are available as well.

Recovery

Alcoholics Anonymous:
http://www.alcoholics-anonymous.org
Provides information regarding Alcoholics Anonymous. AA is a fellowship of men and women who share their experience, strength and hope with each other so they may solve their common problem and help others to recover from alcoholism. There is information on how to identify a problem and how to get help. Since alcoholism affects all people around the alcoholic, information on how to attain help for them is also available.

Al-Anon:
http://www.al-anon.org
Provides information about Al-Anon, a group organized to help the friends and family members of alcoholics to deal with their loved ones' problem. Information on how to get help, including meeting locations and how to attain literature on the topic. A link to the Alateen (Al Anon for teens) website is also available.

Resources

American College Counseling Association:
http://www.collegecounseling.org
Provides information regarding ACCA which supports the practice of college counseling and promotes responsible professional practice to promote communication and exchange among college counselors. The ACCA leads different conferences in an effort to better the counseling services available on college campuses. Many links to other counseling services are found here as well as links to different publications.

Hazeldon Foundation:
http://www.hazeldon.org
Provides information regarding Hazeldon, a nonprofit organization dedicated to helping people recover from alcoholism and other drug addiction. Hazeldon provides both residential and outpatient treatment for people of all ages, programs for families affected by chemical dependency, and training for a variety of professionals. Locations and further information on the treatment facility is listed here as well as.

Recovery Resources:
http://www.recovery.org
Lists different types of treatments available for people who have any type of addiction from alcoholism to overeating. There is online AA help and a recovery resources bookstore.

Safety and Security

Safe Campuses Now:
http://www.uga.edu/~safe-campus
Presents tips on how to be safe on your campus as well as general statistics regarding campus violence. Safe Campuses Now is a crime prevention awareness and education program with the goal of preventing all crime involving college students both on and off campus. There is a crime alert resource page which informs visitors about recent crimes and the still-at-large criminals.

Safety on Campus:
http://www.campussafety.org
Dedicated to assisting campus crime victims in the enforcement of their legal rights. This site informs students about how to be safe and have a successful college experience. Information for parents on how to deal with safety issues is also available. This group has influenced six major legislations all of which are detailed at this site. Crime statistics, safety tips, and bulletin information are also available through this site.

Spring Break

AmeriCorps:
http://www.cns.gov/americorps
Provides information about AmeriCorps programs. AmeriCorps participants teach children to read, help make neighborhoods safer, build affordable homes, and respond to natural dis-

asters. Most AmeriCorps members serve with projects like Habitat for Humanity, the American Red Cross, and Boys and Girls Clubs, and many more local and national organizations. Information on how to get involved is available.

Break Away:
http://www.alternativebreaks.com
Provides information about Alternative Spring Break programs. Alternative breaks are designed to give students an alternate choice for their school breaks rather than going to a resort or staying at home. Opportunities include travel and house building activities as well as environmental clean-up trips, all with the purpose of helping other communities and habitats. Break Away is designed to promote social awareness through service on local, regional, national and international levels.

Campus Outreach Opportunities League
http://www.COOL2SERVE.org/index2.htm
Presents information regarding COOL tranings and workshops related to student community involvement. COOL provides students with an opportunity to connect their personal and local actions with larger movements of people who are serving to better our nation.

Global Volunteers:
http://www.globalvolunteers.org
Provides information regarding Global Volunteers, a private non-profit development organization with the goal of helping to establish a foundation for peace through mutual international understanding. Global Volunteers sends teams of volunteers to live and work with local people on human and economic development projects. Volunteers gain a genuine, firsthand understanding of how other people live day-to-day.

Habitat for Humanity (Campus Chapters):
http://www.habitat.org/CCYP/
Supports students who wish to take an alternative trip during school breaks through Habitat for Humanity. The trips consist of house building for those less fortunate and environmental trips for the restoration of different habitats. Members make a difference for many families and individuals that would otherwise not have the opportunities they are given through this program.

Peace Corps:
http://www.peacecorps.gov/home.html
Provides information about the Peace Corps which works to bring clean water to communities, teach children, help start new small businesses, and stop the spread of AIDS. The volunteers work to develop different countries while getting a better understanding of other cultures and giving those cultures a better understanding of Americans. This site provides the information needed for prospective volunteers as well.

Service-Learning on the World Wide Web:
http://www.csf.colorado.edu/sl/
Supports college students and administrators in the development of service learning programs. Service learning programs are designed to teach students through life experiences

that cannot be taught through a textbook. A master list of all universities involved in these types of programs is available.

Violence

Higher Education Center Against Violence and Abuse:
http://www.mincava.umn.edu/
Lists a wide variety of information on all types of violence and abuse from animal abuse to assault. Each issue has information on how to get help if you need it and other facts on specific violence related issues. There is information for teachers, medical personnel, law enforcement officials and social service providers. There is also a link to different databases with further information on violence and abuse issues.

Partnership Against Violence:
http://www.pavnet.org
Provides information about violence and adolescents that are at risk. Information from seven different Federal agencies is provided. This site also allows violence prevention professionals to communicate through the PAVNET mail group. There is contact information available for those interested in sponsoring a program on violence prevention.

Safe Schools Coalition:
http://www.ed.mtu/safe
Assists colleges and schools in developing safe, healthy, and humane places in which to live and work. Visiting this site allows you to access programs, research, and conference information. This site allows educators, community leaders, the law enforcement community, parents, and students to share ideas to make schools safer, healthier learning environments.

North Dakota Campus Violence Project
http://www.btigate.com/~endabuse
Assists in the prevention of personal violence and promotes healthy and empowered living for college students. Facts on college campus violence are available. Local service information can also be attained.

References

References

1 David Anderson, College Alcohol Survey. Fairfax, VA: George Mason University, 1994.

2 Time magazine, September 8, 1997, p.55

3 Ray Daugherty and Terry O'Bryan, On Campus Talking About Alcohol, (currently called Prime for Life) Lexington, KY: Prevention Research Institute, 1989.

4 Ibid

5 Data generated from Core Alcohol and Drug Survey, Cheryl Presley, Philip Meilman, Rob Tyerla, Jami Leichliter; Core Institute, Southern Illinois University, Carbondale, IL. 1998

6 Lloyd D. Johnston, Patrick M. O'Malley and Jerald G. Bachman, Smoking, Drinking and Illicit Drug Use Among Secondary School Students, College Students and Young Adults, 1975-1991, Vol. II of College Students and Young Adults. Rockville, MD: U.S. Department of Health and Human Services, National Institute on Drug Abuse, 1992.

7 Jane Brody, New York Times, Monday, December 27, 1978.

8 Ibid

9 Center on Addiction and Substance Abuse at Columbia University, Rethinking Rites of Passage: Substance Abuse on America's Campuses, a report by the Commission on Substance Abuse at Colleges & Universities, Joseph Califano, Jr., Chairman, New York, NY, June 1994.

10 Cheryl Presley, Jami Leichliter, and Philip Meilman, Alcohol and Drugs on American College Campuses, A Report to College Presidents, Third in a Series, Southern Illinois University Student Health Program, Carbondale, IL, 1998.

11 Wechsler H. Binge Drinking on American College Campuses: A New Look at an Old Problem. Boston: Harvard School of Public Health, 1995.

12 Elizabeth Parker, Isabel Birenbaum, Rosemary Boyd and Ernest Noble, "Neuropsychologic decrements as a function of alcohol intake in male students," Alcoholism, Clinical and Experimental Research 4: 330-334, 1980.

R. Hannon, C.L. Day, A.M. Butler, A.J. Larson and M. Casey, "Alcohol consumption and cognitive functioning in college students," Journal of Studies of Alcohol, 44: 283-298, 1983.

(Both sources cited in Prime for Life Reference List, see Resources.)

13 Data generated from Core Alcohol and Drug Survey, Cheryl Presley, Philip Meilman, Rob Tyerla, Jami Leichliter; Core Institute, Southern Illinois University, Carbondale, IL. 1998

14 National Highway Traffic Safety Administration, 1998 Traffic Fatality Facts, U.S. Department of Transportation, Washington, DC, July 1998.

[15] Daugherty and O'Bryan, OCTAA, (currently called Prime for Life)1989.

[16] M.S. Gold, "Alcohol, drugs and sexual dysfunction," Alcoholism and Addiction 9:13, 1988. (cited in Raymond Goldberg, Drugs Across the Spectrum, St. Paul, MN: West Publishing Co.: 1994)

[17] Philip Meilman, "Alcohol-Induced Sexual Behavior on Campus," Journal of American College Health 42, July 1993, 27-31.

[18] Ibid

[19] Ibid

[20] Mark Pang, Elizabeth Wells-Parker, and David McMillen, "Drinking Reasons, Drinking Locations, and Automobile Accidents Among Collegians," International Journal of the Addictions 24, no. 3, 215-227, 1989.

[21] Rethinking Rites of Passage.

[22] Hannan KE, Burkhart B. The Topography of Violence in College Men: Frequency and Comorbidity of Sexual and Physical Aggression. Journal of College Student Psychotherapy 1993; 8(3): 219-237.

[23] Roark ML. Conceptualizing Campus Violence: Definitions, Underlying Factors, and Effects. Journal of College Student Psychotherapy 1993; 8(1/2): 1-27

[24] Rethinking Rites of Passage..

[25] Palmer CJ. Violence and Other Forms of Victimization in Residence Halls: Perspectives of Resident Assistants. Journal of College Student Development 1996; 37(3): 268-278.

[26] Lewis Eigen, Alcohol Practices, Policies and Potentials of American Colleges and Universities: An OSAP White Paper, U.S. Department of Health and Human Services, Office for Substance Abuse Prevention, Rockville, MD, 1991.

[27] Roark ML. Conceptualizing Campus Violence: Definitions, Underlying Factors, and Effects. Journal of College Students Psychotherapy 1993; 8(1/2):1-27.

[28] 1995 Audit of Anti-Semitic Incidents. New York: Anti-Defamation League, 1995.

[29] Herek GM. Documenting Prejudice Against Lesbians and Gay Men on Campus: The Yale Sexual Orientation Survey. Journal of Homosexuality 1993; 25(4): 15-30

[30] Rivinus TM, Larimer ME. Violence, Alcohol, Other Drugs, and the College Student. Journal of College Student Psychotherapy 1993; 8(1/2): 71-119.14.

[31] Smith MC. College Liability Resulting From Campus Crime: Resurrection for In Loco Parentis? West's Education Law Report 1990; 59(1): 1-5.

References

32 Infofacts/RESOURCES Sexual Assault and Alcohol and Other Drug Use The Higher Education Center for Alcohol and Other Drug Prevention June 1998)

33 Abbey A. Acquaintance Rape and Alcohol Consumption on College Campuses: How Are They Linked? Journal of American College Health 1991; 39:165-169.)

34 Berkowitz A. College Men as Perpetrators of Acquaintance Rape and Sexual Assault: A Review of Recent Research. Journal of American College Health 1993 40(4):175-181.)

35 Frinter MP, Robinson L. Acquaintance Rape: The Influence of Alcohol, Fraternity Membership, and Sports Team Membership. Journal of Sex Education Therapy 1993; 19(4): 272-284

36 Bausell et al., The Links Among Alcohol, Drugs and Crime; Muehlenhard and Linton, Date Rape and Sexual Aggression. Also Miller, B., and Marshall, J.C. Coercive Sex on the University Campus. Journal of College Student Personnel, 1987

37 Abbey A. Acquaintance Rape and Alcohol Consumption on College Campuses: How Are they Linked? Journal of American College Health 1991; 39: 165-169

38 Bausell et al., The Links Among Alcohol, Drugs and Crime; Muehlenhard and Linton, Date Rape and Sexual Aggression. Also Miller, B., and Marshall, J.C. Coercive Sex on the University Campus. Journal of College Student Personnel, 1987, 28:28-47

39 Abbey A. Acquaintance Rape and Alcohol Consumption on College Campuses: How Are they Linked? Journal of American College Health 1991; 39: 165-169

40 Martin PY. Hummer RA. Fraternities and Rape on Campus. In: Bart PB, Moran K. (eds.) Violence Against Women: The Bloody Footprints. Newbury Park, CA:Sage Publications Inc,; 1993: chap 8.

41 Quackenbush RI. Attitudes of College Men Toward Women and Rape. Journal of College Student Development 1991; 32(4): 376, 377.)

42 Berkowitz A. College Men as Perpetrators of Acquaintance Rape and Sexual Assault: A Review of Recent research. Journal of American College Health 1992; 40(4): 175-181

43 Koss, MP; Gidycz, Caand Wisnewski, The scope of rape: Incidence and prevalence of sexual aggression and victimization in a national sample of higher education students. Journal of Consulting and Clinical Psychology, 1987, 55:162-170;

44 Rape: It Happens to Guys (Flyer) Pennsylvania Coalition Against Rape Harrisburg, PARethinking Rites of Passage.

45 Cynthia KuhnPh.D., Scott Swartzwelder, Ph.D., Wilkie Wilson, Ph.D., Buzzed, W.W.Norton & Co., New York and London;1998

46 These Phases of Drinking are modified from On Campus...Talking About Alcohol and Prime for Life...Risk Reduction for Campuses with the permission of the Prevention Research Institute, Lexington, KY.

47 The "On Campus Talking About Alcohol" Program conducted by the Prevention Research Institute of Lexington, KY contains a complete explanation of this progression.

48 Kaye Fillmore, "Relationship between specific drinking problems in early childhood and middle age; an exploratory 20-year follow-up," Journal for Studies on Alcohol 36: 882-907, 1975.

49 Data generated from Core Alcohol and Drug Survey, Cheryl Presley, Philip Meilman, Rob Tyerla, Jami Leichliter; Core Institute, Southern Illinois University, Carbondale, IL. 1998

50 Remi J. Cadoret, "Psychopathology in adopted-away offspring of biologic parents with antisocial behavior." Archives General Psychiatry, Vol. 35, February, 1978; Remi J. Cadoret and Ann Gath, "Inheritance of alcoholism in adoptees." Journal of Psychology 132: 252-258, 1978. (Cited in Daugherty and O'Bryan, OCTAA.)

51 P. Propping, J. Kruger, and N. Mark, "Genetic Disposition to Alcoholism. An EEG study in alcoholics and their relatives," Human Genetics 59:51-59, 1981; W.F. Gabrielli, S.A. Mednick, J. Volavka, et al. "Electroencephalograms in children of alcoholic fathers," Psychophysiology 19:404-407, 1982. (Cited in Daugherty and O'Bryan, OCTAA.)

52 Marc Schuckit and Vidamantas Rayses, "Ethanol ingestion: differences in blood acetaldehyde concentration, relatives of alcoholics and controls," Science 203: 54-55, 1979. (Cited in Daugherty and O'Bryan, OCTAA.)

53 H.E. Utne, F. Vallo Hansen, K. Winkler and F. Schulsinger, "Alcohol elimination rates in adoptees with and without alcoholic parents," Journal for Studies on Alcohol 38: 1219-1223, 1977. (Cited in Daugherty and O'Bryan, OCTAA.)

54 Lewis Eigen. "Alcohol Practices, Policies and Potentials of American Colleges and Universities." U.S. Public Health Service. 1991. (Cited in Alcohol Issues Insights. Vol. 8, No. 4, 2-3, April 1991.

55 Alcohol Issues Insights. January 1993.

56 H. Wechsler, Binge Drinking on American College Campuses: A New Look at an Old Problem, Boston: Harvard School of Public Health, 1995

57 H. Wechsler, G. Kuh, AE. Davenport, Fraternities and Sororities and Binge Drinking: Results From a National Study of American Colleges, National Association of Student Personnel Administrators 1996. 33(4): 260-279

58 William Celis, "As Fewer Students Drink, Abuse of Alcohol Persists," New York Times, December 31, 1991.

References

59 Frances Harding, <u>Alcohol Problems Prevention/Intervention Programs: Guidelines for College Campuses</u>, State of New York, Division of Alcoholism and Alcohol Abuse, Albany, NY, 1989.

60 Henry Wechsler and Nancy Isaac, "Binge Drinkers at Massachusetts Colleges: Prevalence, Drinking Style, Time Trends and Associated Problems," <u>JAMA 267</u>, no. 21, 1992.

61 Johnson, "Sports and Suds," <u>Sports Illustrated</u>, pp 69-82, August 8, 1988. (Cited in Cornelius and Norton, <u>Images About Alcohol</u>.)

62 Ibid

63 The BACCHUS Peer Education Network: <u>Personal Best, Positive Performance for Athletes</u>, Denver, CO, 1992 (See Resource List.)

64 The College of William and Mary, <u>Alcohol and Drugs vs. Athletic Performance</u>, Williamsburg, VA, 1990.

65 BACCHUS, <u>Personal Best.</u>

66 <u>Bottom Line on Alcohol in Society</u>, Vol. 13, no.1, Spring, 1992, 8-10. (Cited in Cornelius and Norton, <u>Images About Alcohol</u>.)

67 <u>Adweek</u>, 17, April 13, 1992.

68 Emanuel Rubin and Charles Lieber, "Alcohol-induced hepatic injury in nonalcoholic volunteers." <u>The New England Journal of Medicine 278</u>: 869-976, 1968

69 Healthy People 2000, <u>National Health Promotion and Disease Prevention Objectives</u>, September 1990, cited in Office of Substance Abuse Prevention, <u>Bulletin: Take a Look at College Drinking</u>, April 1992.

70 "Confronting Alcohol Problems on College Campuses," Prevention Pipeline, May/June, 1991, 27-31. (Cited in Cornelius and Norton, <u>Images about Alcohol</u>.)

71 Breed, et. al.. <u>Alcohol Advertising in College Newspapers: A Seven Year Followup</u>, In Press, cited Office of Substance Abuse Prevention, op.cit.

72 <u>Rethinking Rites of Passage</u>

73 <u>Wall Street Journal</u>, October 6, 1989, B3. (Cited in Cornelius and Norton, <u>Images about Alcohol</u>.)

74 Prevention Pipeline, U.S. Department of Health and Human Services, January/February, 1992.

75 Statements issued by former Surgeon General Antonia Novello, March 14, 1993.

76 Penny Norton and Sam Cornelius, <u>Images About Alcohol</u>, Midland, MI: Bradford-LaRiviere, Inc., 1991.

77 Data generated from <u>Core Alcohol and Drug Survey</u>, Cheryl Presley, Philip Meilman, Rob Tyerla, Jami Leichliter; Core Institute, Southern Illinois University, Carbondale, IL. 1998

78 Cynthia KuhnPh.D., Scott Swartzwelder, Ph.D., Wilkie Wilson, Ph.D., <u>Buzzed</u>, W.W.Norton & Co., New York and London;1998

79 Henry Wechsler, Ph.D., Bryn Austin, William DeJong; "Secondary Effects of Binge Drinking on College Campuses", <u>The Higher Education Center Bulletin</u>, February, 1996

80 Cheryl Presley, Jami Leichliter, and Philip Meilman, <u>Alcohol and Drugs on American College Campuses, A Report to College Presidents, Third in a Series</u>, Southern Illinois University Student Health Program, Carbondale, IL, 1998.

81 Frank Bumpus, "Everyone may not be getting blasted," <u>The Linfield Review</u>, November 9, 1990.

82 H. Wesley Perkins, Ph.D., Philip W. Meilman. Ph.D., Jami Leichliter, M.A., Jeffrey Cashin, M.A. and Cheryl Presley, Ph.D., "Misperceptions of the Norms for the Frequency of Alcohol and Other Drug Use on College Campuses," <u>Journal of American College Health</u>, Volume 47, May, 1999.

83 Will Keim, Ph.D., <u>The Education of Character</u>; Harc ourt Brace College Publishers, New York, 1995

84 <u>Rethinking Rites of Passage</u>

<u>1000 Remarkable Facts About Alcohol</u> by Richard Erdoes is the source for the historical information regarding alcohol consumption. Permission for use was granted by Smithmark Publications, Inc.; New York, NY.

About the Author

Jim Matthews, M.Ed., is the Special Assistant to the Vice President for Alcohol and Other Drug Programs at Keene State College in New Hampshire. He was a member of the Advisory Board for the United States Department of Education Northeast Regional Center for Drug Free Schools and Communities, is a certified trainer for the Prevention Research Institute and was a participant in the Betty Ford Center Professional in Residence Program. Jim is an approved speaker for the National Collegiate Athletic Association Sports-Sciences Speaker Grant Program. He has conducted presentations and workshops for numerous colleges and professional organizations including the U.S. Coast Guard Academy, Manhattan College, Dean Junior College, Plymouth State College, New England College, Franklin Pierce College, Pennsylvania State University - Mt. Alto, State University of New York - Cortland, Greenfield Community College, the Georgia University System, the Ocean State Center for Law and Citizen Education, the National Association for Campus Activities, and the Network of Colleges and Universities Committed to the Elimination of Alcohol and Drug Abuse. For further information regarding the variety of presentations conducted by Jim Matthews or to order additional copies of Beer, Booze, and Books, contact:

Jim Matthews
Viaticum Press
27 West Ridge Drive
Peterborough, NH 03458
(603) 924-6817
http://www.beerboozebooks.com
bbbjim@monad.net